CONSUMER GUIDE®

CASTLE BOOKS

Contents

This edition published by:
Castle Books
A Division of Book Sales, Inc.
110 Enterprise Avenue
Secaucus, N.J. 07094

Manufactured in the United States of America
1 2 3 4 5 6 7 8 9 10

Library of Congress Catalog Card Number: 80-85353

ISBN: 0-89009-436-5

Principal Author: Richard M. Langworth

Photo Credits: Chevrolet Motor Division, GM Design Staff, GM Photographic, Phil Hall, Bud Juneau, Chris Poole

Cover Design: Frank E. Peiler

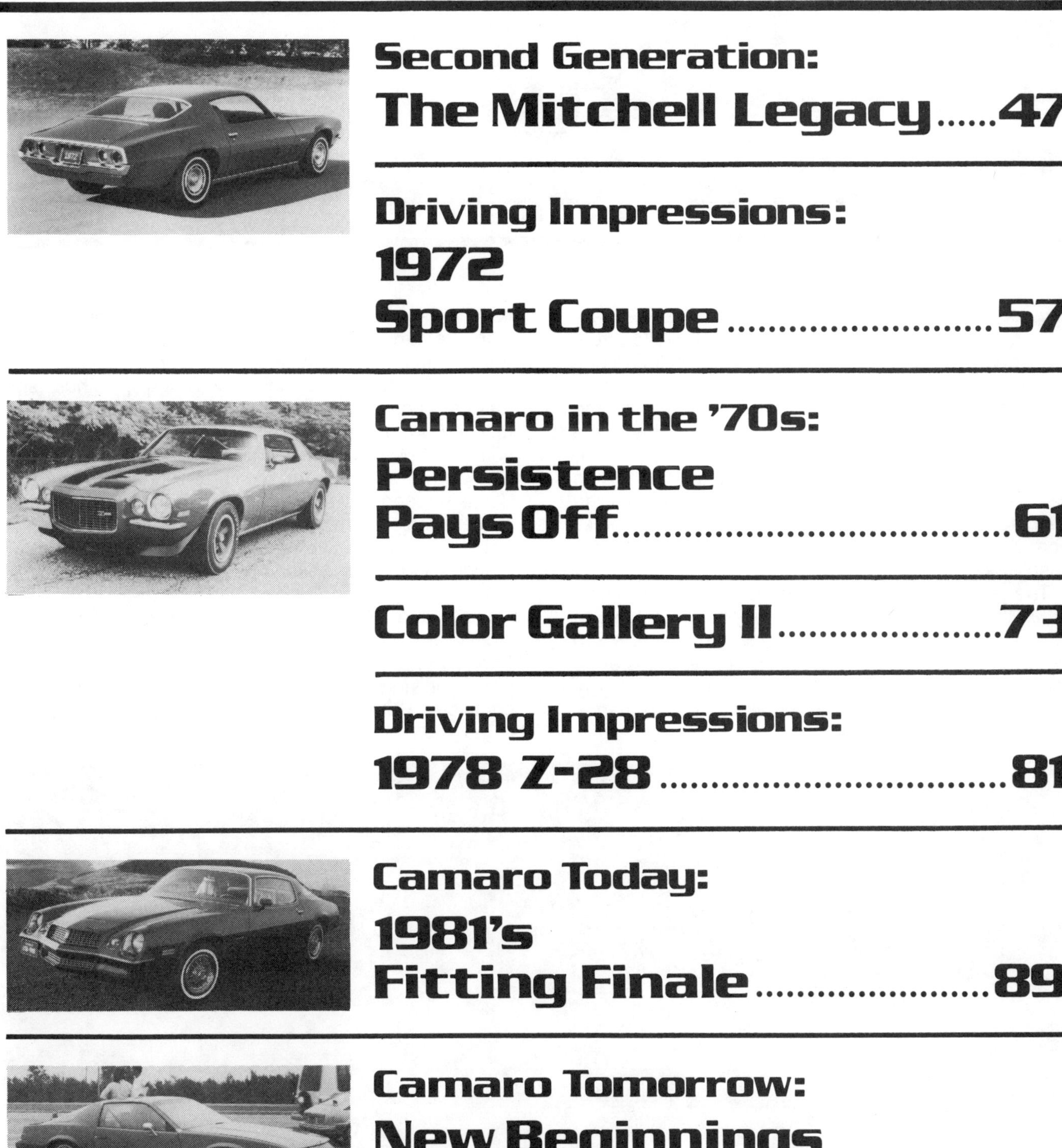

Introduction: Personality Makes It Popular

For car enthusiasts and collectors, the '80s are shaping up as the Chevrolet decade. Aside from the Corvette, which has long been a collector's item, the growing interest in Chevys of all kinds is a new development. For years the dominant force in the old-car hobby was Ford Motor Company, chiefly the Ford Models T, A and V-8, the Continentals, and the Lincoln-Zephyr. Recently, the 1965-66 Mustang has gained a large following, too. But considering all the very desirable collector's items labeled "Chevrolet," Ford will not remain the most popular make for long, if it hasn't already surrendered the title.

The year when Chevy became known for something other than just reliable transportation is not hard to pinpoint. It was 1955, when Ed Cole's remarkable 265 V-8 arrived, wrapped in one of the prettiest bodies of the postwar era. That potent engine also found its way into the Corvette, which has remained a performance car ever since. Today there's not a single undesirable Corvette, and the 1955-57 standard Chevrolet is a red-hot item on the collector market.

Led by these two benchmark Chevys, enthusiasm for other models blossomed in the '70s. Early attention focused on the unique Corvair. It went out of production in 1969, of course, which virtually guaranteed a following of sorts for America's rear-engine compact. But it needed more than that to become a primary interest for over 10,000 people today. More, in this case, was innovative engineering, sprightly performance, and good looks. An ugly Corvair was never built.

In the late '70s, enthusiasts began turning to other Chevy products, notably the potent Super Sport Impalas and Malibus of the mid-'60s. The ever-strong interest in vintage models from the 1930s and '40s also continued. But recently the center of attention in Chevy

1967 Sport Coupe

circles has shifted to a relative latecomer to the fold—the fascinating Camaro.

The Camaro's new-found appeal is a bit surprising. After all, it was, in the beginning, merely a response to the competition—Mustang—not a brand-new idea. Compared to the Corvair, it was conventional in the extreme; compared to the Corvette, it was somewhat less glamorous; compared to the SS 409, it was not truly fast (though the Z-28 was an exception).

What, then, makes the Camaro so sought-after today? Above all, the answer must be "personality." Every Camaro has had it: the RS with its sporty lines and winning performance; the Z-28 with its competitive prowess; the 1970 second-generation coupe with its peerless styling; even the latest 1981 model, which keeps alive the original "ponycar" spirit of the '60s.

Camaro was not designed to be basic transportation, or even to be especially practical. What it was—and still is—was a smooth, powerful, personal road machine, intended mainly for those who enjoyed motoring for sheer pleasure. It had—and still has—looks, speed, handling, comfort, even luxury in some models. It was roomier than an MG, less expensive than a Porsche, more reliable than a Jaguar, and (in some guises) as fast as a Ferrari. And from the first, the Camaro was offered with so many options that you could literally "build" yourself the exact car to fit your personal needs and tastes. Today, you can probably find your ideal among older-model Camaros on the collector market, if you're patient enough.

That the Camaro continues with its original character is remarkable in view of what happened in the '70s. That was the decade that saw oil shortages, dollar-a-gallon gas, and government regulations change the shape of the American car—not to mention the end of the Camaro's early competitors. Today, all that's left from the ponycar era is this handsome Chevy and its Pontiac counterpart, the Firebird. But happily, the finishing touches are being put on their successors even as this is being written.

Part of the Camaro's special magic is that the car has remained faithful to a theme of sporty, affordable personal transportation. But its sheer endurance, its survival in a changing world, is also an important part of its mystique. It's still part of the Chevrolet lineup, and seems likely to remain so. This means Camaro continues to win new fans all the time, while Corvair, for example, does not. Camaro lovers now include not only those who bought a new one yesterday, but also those who, in their younger days, might have owned a '67 Rally Sport or a '70 Z-28, who remembered what those cars were like, and who have treated themselves to "one like I had."

This book is dedicated to Camaro enthusiasts of all ages and owners of all models. Here you'll find insight into the car's three design generations: 1967-69, 1970-81, and the all-new '82. You'll also find driving impressions of four significant examples so you can feel what each is like from the place where it counts most—behind the wheel. In these pages are Camaro's past, present, and its promising future—a future which is still secure in a time of uncertainty.

So, settle back and enjoy. And as you do, remember the traditional toast of Bugatti enthusiasts, which is equally apt for Camaro and one of the best we know: *Viva la marque!*

1971 Z-28

Early prototype for second-generation Camaro

1980 Z-28

First Generation: Challenges and Choices

Some people think that if it hadn't been for the Mustang there would have never been a Camaro. This is something of an oversimplification and misses the real point. By late 1966, when the Camaro was introduced, there was already a high demand for such cars, and it was still growing. GM was simply responding. True, that buyer demand had been generated largely by the Mustang, but it actually started developing long before Ford's ponycar arrived.

Interest in sporty, close-coupled compacts that could seat two comfortably and four in a pinch probably goes back to 1956. That was the year Studebaker fielded its first Hawks—nimble, fast road machines that looked different and performed considerably better than the average family sedan. For 1958, Ford punched its two-seat Thunderbird out to a four-seat configuration, which also introduced a radical new body design that met with overwhelming acceptance. GM replied with the Pontiac Grand Prix in 1962 and the stunning four-place Buick Riviera the following year. Similar concepts followed, such as Oldsmobile's Toronado of 1966. The race was on.

Until Mustang, however, four-seat "personal" cars had been mainly upper-price luxury models. But stylists and engineers at General Motors were thinking about something in the lower-price class a good six years before the Mustang debuted in early 1964. Pontiac designer Bob Porter, for example, told author Michael Lamm,* "As early as 1958, I remember a four-passenger, sporty type car of the general size and weight class of the Mustang being worked on in an advanced studio. In the early '60s, similar cars were developed from time to time. Everyone wanted to do one, but at the time there was really no corporate interest."

The first low-priced "personal" car that made a hit with the public was created almost by accident, when Chevrolet added bucket seats to its Corvair sports coupe late in the 1960 model year. Compared to the more cheaply furnished 500 and 700 versions, the new Corvair Monza 900 was an eye-popper. It offered a color-keyed interior, comfortable vinyl bucket seats, and (in 1961) the option of a four-speed manual gearbox. Monzas sold like hot coffee on a cold morning. Soon they were outselling all other Corvair models combined. Ford and Chrysler, taking due note, rushed to equip their Falcon and Valiant compacts with deluxe interiors, consoles, bucket seats and floor shifts. This trend ultimately led, of course, to the Falcon-based Mustang, and its success is well-known: 100,000 units sold in the first six months, over half a million in the first year.

But the Mustang's introduction caused no immediate reaction at GM, which took a "wait-and-see" attitude. For awhile, GM felt that its forthcoming fully restyled 1965 Corvair, with a sophisticated four-wheel independent suspension and rear-mounted engine offering up to 180 bhp, would easily outsell the more pedestrian Mustang. It didn't. By August 1964—only four months after Ford's "quarter horse" appeared—GM had decided to begin development of a product much more like it. It would have a front engine, rear drive, an attractive base price, and would be offered with a large number of extra-cost items so buyers could "tailor" the car to suit their individual preferences. This last provision was most significant. Mustang had demonstrated that a comprehensive options list would allow a basic, inexpensive package to serve as an economy runabout, sporty compact, or a relatively luxurious "personal" car, all at the same time. Despite its many good points, the Corvair never had this kind of versatility. This was one reason why it never outsold the economy Falcon. Another was character. Corvair and its interesting engineering appealed mainly to a fairly small group of knowledgeable enthusiasts, not the much greater number of "mainstream" buyers attracted to the Falcon's anvil-like simplicity.

Early on, it was determined that Chevy's Mustang-fighter would be based on off-the-shelf components shared with a "volume" family model. Product planning and production considerations decreed that the new car should relate closely to the Chevy II, which was set to be completely restyled and re-engineered for 1968. The original Chevy II had also failed to outsell the Falcon, but the 1968 and later models (known simply as Nova from 1969 on) were very successful.

The job of shaping what would become the Camaro was handed to the GM Design Center's Chevrolet Studio Two under Henry C. Haga. The chain of command—important because all echelons had a role in determining Camaro styling—stretched from Haga to David M. Holls, Charles M. Jordan, Irwin W. Rybicki,

Airbrush rendering (circa 1963) for Project XP-836, the eventual Camaro

July 1962 clay model preceeded formal start of XP-836, resembles '66 Toronado.

Note tunnelback roof and fender exhaust ports of above clay. Intriguingly, model bears "Cobra" emblems.

and on to design vice-president William L. Mitchell. Mitchell never liked the first-generation Camaro. "It wasn't worth a damn," he remarked to *Car Classics* magazine in 1978, "There were too many people involved." In his view, the styling suffered because the car had to be designed with an eye to sharing components. Dave Holls, then Chevrolet group chief designer, noted two areas where the styling was compromised for just this reason: cowl height and hood length.

The Camaro project was designated "F-car" early on. As its general styling inspiration it looked to the Chevrolet Super Nova, a show car first seen at the New York Auto Show in early 1964, shortly before the

Another early XP-836 clay bore "Vega" script.

Stylists did many renditions of this basic shape in 1964.

Camaro's bodyside peak was already evident in September 1964.

Designers were denied a fastback, but developed the style anyway. From October 1964.

production Mustang was introduced. The Super Nova was a clean, smooth-lined coupe, but was not particularly stunning. It merely expressed GM's mid-'60s styling philosophy. "Fluidity" is how one staffer explained it: "If you take a heavy wire frame and bend it into the basic 3-dimensional outline of the car you want, then stretch thin canvas over the frame, and if you finally blow compressed air gently into the bottom of the canvas envelope, you get a very natural, free-flowing, unartificial body shape. This fluid form showed up most strikingly in the 1965 crop of General Motors cars."

The emphasis on roundness—ironically, so well-expressed in the ill-fated second-generation Corvair—contrasts sharply with the square-rigged lines of contemporary Fords. Seen in profile, the '67 Camaro was smoother, more flowing; that year's Mustang more angular and abrupt. The two car companies' different approaches are hard to compare objectively. Critics agreed that the Mustang's overall look benefitted because of its longer hood, while some stylists felt the Camaro, with its shorter hood, looked too much like a Corvair for its own good. Still, the balance of professional judgment is on the side of the Camaro. And significantly, the Mustang's styling became noticeably more "fluid" in its succeeding design generations.

Henry Haga summarized the GM styling concept as applied to the Camaro: "We felt very strongly about reducing design to its simplest form, using only one peak down each body side, interrupted by accented wheel arches. The profile of the car also was very simple, using the classic approach of crowned fender lines, with their high points directly above the accented wheel arches. We purposefully avoided any contrived design lines and superfluous detail. Even the execution of the wide, horizontal-loop front end and grille, with its hidden headlamps in the Rally Sport variant, was as pure in concept as we could make it."

Interior design was directed by George Angersbach, a specialist in Chevy's smaller cars—Corvette, Corvair, Nova, and the soon-to-be Camaro. Angersbach remembers that the Camaro (and Corvair) borrowed heavily from the dashboard design of the all-new 1968 Corvette, which was being styled at the same time. This layout featured two large round dials set squarely in front of the driver. However, it presented a problem because the size of the dials left little space ahead of the steering wheel, where sporting drivers might want a bank of auxiliary gauges. A compromise was suggested by interior stylist Sue Vanderbilt, who created a three-dial cluster to mount atop an optional center console. This treatment was continued, using a staggered or "sawtooth" four-dial cluster for 1968 and '69. The console wasn't the best place to put the gauges for easy viewing, but at least it *was* a place to put them.

The Camaro's body was one of the first at GM to be seriously evaluated in a wind tunnel. In those days, GM used the facilities of the Ling-Temco-Vought Aircraft Company in Dallas, Texas. (In 1980, the automaker officially opened its own wind tunnel at the GM Tech Center in Warren, Michigan.) Although the tests were not conducted until the styling was almost finalized, it proved to have excellent aerodynamic characteristics—a tribute to the design team. The only changes necessary were mild modifications to the front fenders and the front pan under the bumper.

One thing the designers didn't get with the first-generation Camaro was a fastback body style. They

Late-'64 interior mock-up shows Corvette influence.

Near-final '67 interior. Staffer holds console gauge pod.

Two-seat roadster was tried but rejected on cost grounds.

March 1966 sport-wagon clay. Style was nixed to keep costs down.

Factory drawing shows Camaro's unique front sub-frame. Cowl was shared with '68 Chevy II.

did do one in mock-up form as a potential answer to the Mustang 2+2. But management insisted on just two models, a coupe and convertible, mostly for cost reasons. Farther behind in the running—but still present in the minds and drawings of the designers for awhile—were a two-seat cabriolet and a smooth, two-door sport-wagon. The consensus is that these extensions were also precluded by cost. GM was, after all, attempting to match the Mustang's $2500 base price.

A critical engineering decision made right at the first was to use a front sub-frame in combination with unit construction for the Camaro—and, in due course, the 1968 Nova. This was a fairly unique approach in that the sub-frame was isolated from the body by rubber inserts or "biscuits," as the engineers called them. This

Management preview model from August 1965. Note small wheels, Panther fender emblem.

Lower stance, wider track were last-minute changes.

Panther name was discarded, as were round taillights.

Torsional vibration showed up in convertible running prototypes, was cured with "cocktail shakers."

technique had been refined on costlier European unit-body cars, including various Mercedes-Benz models and the larger Opels, but Camaro was the first application of it for a low-price American car. The compromise was highly effective. Unit construction techniques allowed more passenger and luggage space than a body designed for a separate full chassis. The relatively exotic rubber mounts gave a smoother, quieter ride than cars with sub-frames bolted directly to the main bodyshell, like early-'60s Chrysler products. (In fact, the problem of isolating road noise with a front sub-frame was one of the reasons Imperials of the period stayed with a separate frame.)

The rear suspension was a less happy arrangement. Chevy adopted single-leaf (Mono-Plate) springs used successfully on the Chevy II and Olds Toronado, but

Running prototypes, built from cobbled-up Chevy IIs, in winter 1965

this resulted in considerable axle tramp in hard acceleration with the larger V-8 engines. Several band-aid engineering measures were tried after the first Camaros came off the line. For 1967, the big-engine models were fitted with traction bars, and the '68s had staggered shocks. These alterations reduced the axle tramp tendency, but a more sophisticated rear suspension should have been attempted. Again, however, a tight budget was the limiting factor.

Another early Camaro flaw was rear-end bottoming under heavy loads. This resulted from a decision made during executive reviews of the final prototypes. Originally, the standard Camaro was slated to ride on 13-inch wheels. But this, along with the high cowl, gave the prototypes an ungainly, "small-wheeled" look. To satisfy the sales department, which wanted a more aggressive appearance, engineers lowered the car and substituted 14-inch wheels and tires. The lowering contributed to the bottoming. This problem was never entirely cured on the 1967 models, though rear suspension travel was increased on the '68s to get around it.

One other interesting engineering trick was the use of what GM men called "cocktail shakers"—harmonic shock absorbers located at each corner in Camaro convertibles. Their purpose was to control torsional vibration, which Chevrolet testers encountered in early shakedowns of the running prototypes. The tuned shockers helped make the ragtop a very tight package. This was not a feature unique to Camaro, though. It was also used on Thunderbird and Lincoln convertibles as early as 1961, and on open 1965-69 Corvairs.

Camaro engines were shared with the concurrent Chevelle. Chevy's 230 cubic-inch six (140 bhp) was standard, with a 250-cid six (155 bhp) optional. Then came a long line of V-8s, commencing with 210- and 265-bhp 327s, and running on to the big 396-cid, 375-bhp L-78 with four-barrel carburetors and 11:1 compression. This array of powerplants put Camaro firmly in the Mustang league. It was a car the buyer could equip to suit his or her preferences—exactly what GM wanted it to be. Incidentally, the Camaro had strong appeal for both sexes: female buyers numbered one out of four.

Chevrolet probably should have offered "courses in Camaro" to its customers in 1967—it certainly did to Chevy salesmen—so they could make sense of the enormous option list. It has been suggested that Detroit's practice of offering a plethora of optional extras, which began in the '60s, contributed to its quality-control problems and sales losses to the imports, most of which come fully equipped. Nevertheless, options was the way to go in 1967, and was a big reason for the Camaro's early success. As our tables show, it was possible to build virtually any kind of car you wanted, as long as you had spent enough time reviewing the accessories sheets.

The Camaro was the subject of extensive sneak previews and rumors months before its official introduction. This probably took away some potential sales from Corvair. But by that time, GM was heavily committed to its Mustang-beater, and had started to downplay the rear-engined compact in the wake of widespread controversy over its safety. The Camaro formally arrived in dealerships nationwide on September 21, 1966. Chevy explained that the new car's name was taken from an old French word meaning "companion" or "pal." Chevy even produced a photostat of an old French dictionary as proof. Despite its unfamiliar name, the Camaro sold well. For 1967, Chevrolet regained first rank in model year production, which it had lost to Ford in 1966. Volume was 2.2 million vehicles—and fully 10 per cent were Camaros. Camaro didn't beat Mustang's sales, which were lower in '67 than in '65 and '66. They would drop even faster as Camaro began to hit its stride in 1968 and '69.

The second-edition '68 Camaro was marked by only minor changes. Instant identification was provided by

1967 SS coupe with RS equipment. Deep-dish "tulip" wheel covers were popular on SS cars.

the new side marker lights mandated for all cars that year by the government. Other changes were less evident. In common with other '68 Chevys (except Corvair) Camaro acquired flow-through "Astro Ventilation," thus doing away with "no-draft" quarter vents in the doors. It also adopted a peaked and silver (instead of flat and black) grille, and oblong (instead of round) parking lights. The tailights were still oblong, with separate red and white (backup) lenses on the standard versions, and a quartet of square red lenses

Full-width RS grille had SS insignia with that option.

Under-bumper backup lights identified RS-equipped '67s.

Distinctive "bumblebee" hood stripe came with the SS package, but not the RS.

Style Trim exterior included wheel opening and rocker moldings.

March 1966 sport-wagon clay. Note revised roof.

Mid-1966 clay for 1968 restyle.

Moving further afield, possibly toward '69.

Opposite side of clay at left. Note vinyl top.

Stylists still played with two-seaters in fall 1966.

Fender "speed streaks" appeared early in '69 program.

A fastback answer to Mustang 2+2....

....many versions were tried in early '67.

An idea for '69, more radical than what emerged.

Close to final '69 grille. Note hood scoops.

Sawtooth taillamps, square exhaust ports didn't make it.

(separate backup lamps below the bumper) for the RS.

The 1968 SS-396 received additional detailing which made it stand out from the rest of the line—a black-painted back panel and a new hood with fake air intakes. The SS package now included front disc brakes as standard equipment, and offered a choice of three different striping patterns, including a "pulsating" set of color bands going from dark to light before merging into the body color. Most RPOs (Regular Production Options) and the drivetrain lineup remained virtually the same as in '67.

The first generation was changed considerably for 1969, its last year. It would also be an extra-long model year because the new 1970 Camaro was delayed until spring of that year. The engine lineup (see chart) was shuffled, as the 327 V-8 gave way to a new 307, and the 350-cid L-65 unit replaced the high-performance 327. Four-wheel disc brakes, offered for '68 on the Z-28 mainly to give the racing versions better stopping power, now became optional for all models. Federal bumper regulations (then restricted to bumper height, not crash resistance) were in effect, and Camaro was right up to date with optional Endura compressible bumpers. There were more vinyl roof colors, and two-tone paint was offered.

The classic Mercedes-Benz 300SL sports car of the late '50s and early '60s has inspired the design of many Detroit cars, some of which actually benefitted from its example. The Camaro certainly did: its front wheel cutouts were more square, and gained speed streaks echoing the heavily emphasized "brows," of the Mercedes. These swept straight back from both front and rear wheels to give a look of forward motion. (One 300SL item probably did *not* appear in production: simulated air vents behind the front wheels. This was proposed for the '68 Rally Sport and some factory photographs show it, but it was likely scrapped at the last minute.)

The "face" of the '69 car was also altered as much as possible without major sheetmetal changes. The grille was set farther back in its opening, more strongly vee'd than before, and got a big eggcrate pattern. On Rally Sport models, the headlamps remained hidden when off, but their covers now had three glass "ribs," which allowed some light to shine through if the doors failed to retract. (One might have thought that, with this sort of fail-safe device, the Camaro used a troublesome British-made electrical system. It's too bad the Triumph TR7 doesn't have a similar provision for its pop-up lights.)

The late '60s saw the height of the ponycar craze, as all the major makes brought out short-wheelbase, two-passengers-plus-two-in-a-pinch sporty compacts. Everyone was after the market that the Mustang had exploited so early—Mercury with its Cougar, Dodge with its Charger, Rambler with its ill-advised Marlin, Pontiac with its Firebird, and Plymouth with its Barracuda. The latter was fully restyled for 1967, adding another low-priced challenge to the Mustang, though it didn't approach either Mustang or Camaro in sales. What is most interesting is how Camaro production

1967 Sport Coupe and SS convertible.

Camaro Major Options

Like Mustang, Camaro was successful because it was offered with a wide variety of options. This allowed the purchaser to "customize" the car in an almost infinite number of ways—economical, sporty, high-performance, or various combinations of these. Here is a list of the main RPOs (Regular Production Options) that made it all possible.

INTERIOR
Standard trim: Solid-color vinyl bucket seats, carpeting, molded door panels, applied armrests, exposed door handles.
Custom trim (RPO-Z-87): vinyl bucket seats with contrast striping, carpeting, embossed seat and door trim, color-keyed accents, padded door panels, built-in armrests, recessed door handles, $94.80.
RPO
A-01 tinted glass, $30.55
A-02 tinted windshield, $21.00
A-31 power windows, $100.10
A-85 deluxe front shoulder belts, $26.00
AL-4 Strato-back bench seat, $26.35
AL-67 fold-down rear seatback with carpeted back, $31.60
AS-1 front shoulder belts, $23.00
AS-2 twin front seat headrests, $52.70
C-50 rear-window defroster, $21.10
C-60 Four-Season air conditioning, $356.00
D-33 remote-control exterior mirror, $9.00
D-55 tunnel console with glovebox, ashtray and courtesy light, $47.70
K-30 Cruise-Master speed control, $50.05
N-33 tilt-adjustable steering column, $42.15
N-34 walnut-grain steering wheel, $32.00
N-40 deluxe steering wheel, $7.00
U-17 three-dial gauge cluster (V-8 only), $79.00
U-57 8-Track stereo tape player (radio required) $128.10
U-63 AM pushbutton radio, $57.00
U-69 AM/FM pushbutton radio, $133.80
U-35 electric clock, $15.80
U-80 rear speaker, $14.00
Other Interior Options
Underhood insulation, rear seat armrests with ashtrays, molded trunk mat, courtesy lights (coupe), Special Interior (chromed plastic windshield pillar moldings, chromed inside roof rail moldings, bright-trim pedal pads.)

EXTERIOR
Standard: plain body (without pinstriping or chrome accents), painted steel wheels with hubcaps, blackwall tires.
RPO
C-06 power convertible top, $52.70
C-08 vinyl roof (black or fawn), $73.75
N-96 mag-style wheel covers, $73.75
P-12 Rally wheels (five-slot), $53.50
PO-1 deep-dish wheel covers, $21.10
PO-2 simulated wire wheel covers, $73.75
Z-21 Style Trim Group (pinstriping, anodized-aluminum wheel cutout moldings, stainless-steel drip moldings), $40 coupe, $30 convertible.
Z-22 Rally Sport (RS) package (hidden headlamps in full-width grille, under-bumper parking lights, full taillights with separate backup lamps, RS emblems, pinstriping, rocker/drip/wheel cutout moldings, black-painted rocker bottoms), $105.35

MECHANICAL
RPO
F-21/41 heavy-duty suspension (for SS or with 275-bhp 327 V-8), $10.55
G-80 Positraction limited-slip differential, $42.15
J-50 power brakes (vacuum assist), $42.15
J-52 11-inch ventilated front disc brakes, $79.00
J-65 sintered metallic brake linings, $37.90
N-40 power steering, $84.30
N-44 quick-ratio steering (manual or power), $15.80
Choice of rear axle ratios, $2.00
Tires: standard 7.35×14 blackwall; optional 7.35×14 whitewall, D70-14 Wide-Oval red stripe on 6-inch wheels.

Equipping Your Camaro

Here are three examples of how the option book could be used to create three entirely different Camaros, each with its own distinctive personality:

THE ECONOMY CAMARO
Comfort, Convenience, and Appearance: Standard coupe (without pinstriping or chrome accents), painted wheels with hubcaps and blackwall tires, standard vinyl bucket seats and carpeting, standard molded door panels with applied armrests, optional AM pushbutton radio. **Engine:** base 230-cid six with 140 bhp. **Transmission:** standard three-speed manual with column shift. **Price:** approximately $2550, plus destination and prep charges.

THE LUXURY CAMARO
Comfort, Convenience and Appearance: Convertible, RS option, simulated wire wheel covers, tinted glass, power side windows, Custom interior, deluxe front shoulder belts, fold-down rear seatback, twin front seat headrests, air conditioning, remote-control exterior mirror, tunnel console, power convertible top, speed control, tilt-adjustable steering column, deluxe steering wheel, AM/FM pushbutton stereo radio with rear speaker, electric clock, power steering. **Engine:** 350-cid V-8 with 295 bhp. **Transmission:** Turbo Hydra-Matic. **Price:** approximately $4460, plus destination and prep charges.

THE PERFORMANCE CAMARO
Comfort, Convenience and Appearance: Coupe with Z-28 option, RS package (RPO Z-22), mag-style wheel covers, front shoulder belts, twin front seat headrests, tunnel console, walnut-grained steering wheel, three-dial gauge cluster, AM/FM radio, electric clock. **Functional:** F-41 heavy-duty suspension, Positraction, front disc brakes, sintered metallic rear brake linings, power brakes, quick-ratio power steering, Wide-Oval red stripe tires, oversize wheels, rear spoiler, four-speed manual transmission. **Engine:** Z-28 302-cid V-8 with 290 bhp (advertised). **Price:** approximately $4000, plus destination and prep charges.

Waikiki show Camaro made the rounds in 1967.

Fiberglass model for '68. Dummy fender vents....

....appeared in factory photos, but not in production.

The 1968 convertible with Style Trim exterior

Caribe show car from '68 had pickup-style cargo box.

The 1968 Sport Coupe with Style Trim exterior

The 1968 SS-350. Note rear lip spoiler.

A non-RS 1969 Super Sport

The 1969 Sport Coupe

"Peekaboo" headlight doors adorned '69 RS grille.

Camaro Engine Options 1967-69

Engine	cid	bore × stroke (in.)	bhp @ rpm (gross)	C.R. (:1)	carb (bbls)	Available: 1967	1968	1969
six	230	3.88 × 3.25	140 @ 4400	8.5	1	x	x	x
six	250	3.88 × 3.53	155 @ 4200	8.5	1	x	x	x
V-8	302	4.00 × 3.01	290 @ 5800	11.0	4	x	x	x
V-8	307	3.88 × 3.25	200 @ 4600	9.0	2			x
V-8	327	4.00 × 3.25	210 @ 4600	8.75	2	x	x	x
V-8	327	4.00 × 3.25	275 @ 4800	10.0	4	x	x	
V-8	350	4.00 × 3.48	250 @ 4800	9.0	2			x
V-8	350	4.00 × 3.48	295 @ 4800	10.25	4	x	x	
V-8	350	4.00 × 3.48	300 @ 4800	10.25	4			x
V-8	396	4.09 × 3.76	325 @ 4800	10.25	4	x	x	x
V-8	396	4.09 × 3.76	350 @ 5200	10.25	4			x
V-8	396	4.09 × 3.76	375 @ 5600	11.0	4	x	x	x
V-8	427	4.25 × 3.76	425 @ 5600	11.0	3 × 2			x

remained almost stable from 1967 through 1969, while Mustang figures dropped steadily. By the end of the decade, Camaro was rapidly closing on the original ponycar:

Model Year	Camaro	Mustang	Barracuda
1967	220,917	472,121	62,534
1968	235,151	317,404	45,412
1969	243,095	299,824	32,987

Sales figures for cars like the Firebird and Cougar show that all other challengers were merely chipping away at Mustang, while Camaro gamely held its own profitable market share.

'69 restyle was simple but effective. This is the RS coupe.

Heavy dash woodgrain was rejected as "1970" change.

How did the "low-price three's" ponycar contenders compare? Camaro and Barracuda were certainly more up to date in styling than the Mustang. Yet none of the three had a clear performance lead over the others. Each car was, as *Road & Track* magazine put it, "basically a compact sedan with a stylish body, with all the virtues and vices of the typical American sedan. True, each can be ordered with things like improved steering, braking, handling, instrumentation, etc. But in each case these things aren't a fundamental part of the concept. None of them offers anywhere near the best present-day standards in braking or handling. Each of them is a very plain car in standard form, and the options necessary to bring them up to the relatively simple form in which we tested them make them fairly expensive cars."

Missing in this analysis is the fact that European 2+2s were designed for the needs of a very much smaller, more highly specialized market. As a result, the volume necessary for a firm like Ferrari or Mercedes-Benz to break even on such expensive products was a lot lower than for a mass-production U.S. model.

Camaro was selected to pace the Indianapolis 500 twice in three years—1967 and 1969—so it must have impressed *some* people who liked to go fast. But not the editors of *Road & Track:* "The Camaro is, frankly, a disappointment. Chevrolet has been an engineering leader in the past, and we assumed that if they had years in which to develop a car, they might reasonably be expected to surpass the Mustang rather than just equal it."

In truth, that's just what happened. As proof, consider the Z-28—which we do in the following pages.

**Quotations cited (except those of William L. Mitchell) are used with permission of Michael Lamm as published in his book "The Great Camaro," ©1978-79, Lamm-Morada Publishing Co., Box 7607, Stockton, CA 95207.*

Camaros were hot on the drag strip, too. This '69 is shown at the 1973 NHRA Nationals. John Legenfelter won his class.

Prototype for "1970" continuation of '69 style

Note split hood stripe on "1970" styling model.

Racing great Jim Rathman with the 1969 Indy Pace Car

Camaros sold through early 1970 were unchanged from '69s.

Driving Impressions: 1967 Sport Coupe

In 1967, the Camaro was sometimes described by automotive journalists as a Detroit alternative to imported sports cars. Yet oddly enough, hardly anybody bothered to test one equipped along the lines of a European GT. Lack of publicity didn't hurt the six-cylinder cars—at least in the beginning. From 50,000 to 65,000 were sold each year during the first generation, accounting for about one in every four sales. Considering that the emphasis in auto magazines and in GM showrooms was on the V-8s, the sixes made a rather good showing.

With the arrival of the heavier, coupe-only, second

Though ignored by the press, the six-cylinder Camaro rivalled many European sports cars.

generation for 1970½, six-cylinder sales plummeted. The best year they've recorded since then was 1977 when 38,000 found customers. Yet that was only 17 percent of that year's total production. Only after the Arab oil embargo of 1973-74 (and the resultant demand for more economical cars) did six-cylinder Camaros become more popular. Their relative rarity in the early '70s was due to several factors.

First, gasoline was artificially cheap in the U.S. through 1974 and beyond due to government price policy. As a result, most buyers opted for the thirstier V-8s. Second, the all-new 1970½ models were more softly sprung and more luxurious than their predecessors. A convertible was missing, partly because of the trend away from ragtops and toward air conditioning. No more than 38,000 of the 1967-early 1970 Camaros were ordered with "air." By 1974, that number had risen to near 80,000, and better than half the 1977 cars had the option. But it wasn't until 1975 that you could even *get* a six-cylinder Camaro with air conditioning. One reason was that dealers usually urged customers to team A/C with a V-8. They were concerned that "air" would leave the car underpowered with a six.

Nevertheless, a properly set-up six-cylinder Camaro can be a mighty pleasing package—in coupe or convertible form. And it didn't cost much, either—about $3300 for the one you see here. That was a pretty good deal back in 1967. By today's standards, it's positively mind-boggling.

Our subject car is almost ideally equipped for those customers who might have bought an MG or Triumph but didn't because there wasn't enough room for extra passengers or luggage. This Camaro has the optional 250-cid six with 155 horsepower, which provided a welcome performance boost over the standard 230-cid unit at little cost in fuel mileage. This willing engine is

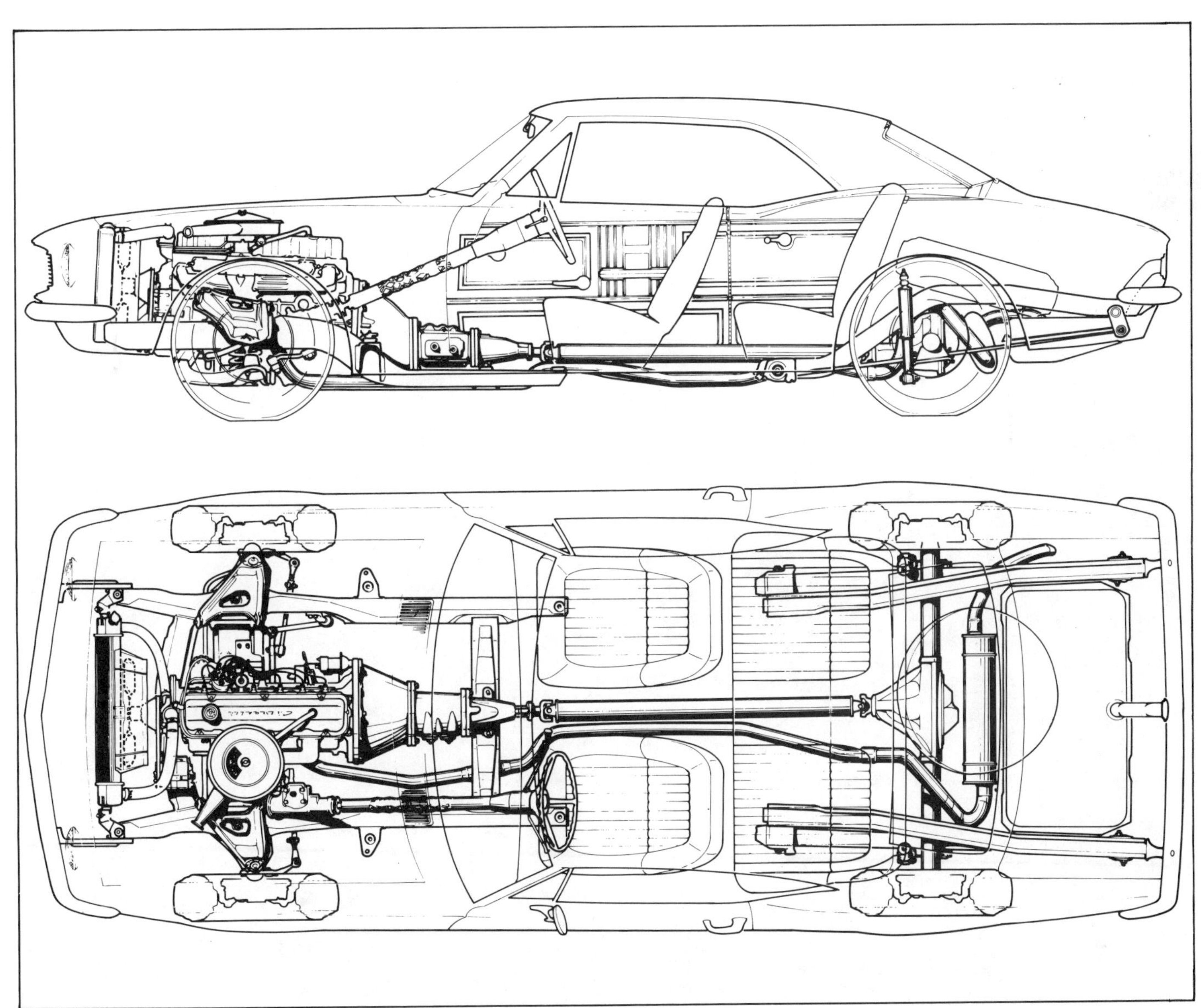

Side elevation (above) and plan view (below) drawings show why Camaro's back seat was for occasional use only.

Though not a lightweight, 250-cid six gave Camaro better handling balance than the heavier V–8s.

hooked to an all-synchro gearbox, with four, fairly widely spaced ratios, and the optional 3.55:1 "performance" rear axle ratio. (The standard gearing for both sixes was 3.08:1; the "economy" cog was 2.73:1.) While the 3.55 cut down a little on top speed, it provided low-end performance which rivaled that of, say, a Triumph TR4. And, considering the Camaro weighed about 3000 pounds (19.4 pounds per horsepower), it had very decent acceleration in this form.

The Rally Sport option is our idea of the perfect trim scheme for the Camaro—neither too plain like the standard-trim version, nor too flashy like the SS. Briefly, it altered the car's appearance by means of concealed headlights set in a full-width grille, parking and backup lights mounted below the bumpers, lower bodyside moldings with black finish underneath, bright moldings around the wheel openings and along the beltline, and discreet "RS" script and emblems.

A '67 convertible shows off its Custom Interior and optional console.

Contemporary factory photo shows an "economy" Camaro in an appropriately youth-oriented setting.

The 1967 model is also our choice as the best styled Camaro from the early years. Detroit is frequently criticized for messing up a basically good design just for the sake of change. The Camaro's cosmetic surgery for 1968 and '69 was minor, to be sure, but it wasn't necessary. Despite Bill Mitchell's suggestion that this is a committee design, we like it fine—especially the convertible. (The committee must have been a good one.) It was sporty yet practical for a car of its day, and it's still well-suited for 1981 driving conditions. And who would complain about this kind of performance combined with 22 miles to a gallon of regular?

Your first impression on stepping inside (well, actually it's more like swinging in) is things seem very snug, a trait of late-'60s American coupes. The back seat, by the way, is strictly "for emergency use only." Legroom for adults exists in name only, and

Tunnel console could be ordered with or without the extra-cost Custom Interior.

Design chief Mitchell called it a committee car, but the first generation shape still pleases more than a decade later.

riding more than a dozen miles back there is guaranteed to wrinkle your designer jeans. Up front, the vinyl buckets of the Custom Interior are well proportioned and comfortable. Unfortunately, there is no rake adjustment for the seatbacks, and drivers with long legs would probably complain about lack of sufficient fore/aft seat travel. The big main instruments are quite legible, though their curious cone-shaped lenses produce a little distortion. All the controls—as the British say—fall readily to hand, obligatory in this sort of car. So, notch the four-speed into first, and move out.

You'll be impressed immediately. Repeated 0-60 mph runs hardly ever varied between 12.5 and 14 seconds—and this with a *six,* mind you. In standing-

Six-cylinder Camaro makes a practical-and interesting-alternative to today's "econoboxes" for everyday driving.

start quarter-mile times, the Camaro matches the Triumph almost exactly. That's fine, because the TR4 is (was) a near ideal compromise between performance and economy. The Chevy couldn't get through the quarter before the upshift to third was called for, but the shifts ran through quickly and didn't seriously effect our times. We were only able to estimate the top speed: 95 mph. You might well be able to exceed three figures with a numerically lower axle ratio—an academic exercise anyway on 55-mph-limited American roads.

The 250 six cost only $26.35 extra back in '67, but was worth its weight in gold (or nowadays, at least copper). Its torque peak comes at a mere 1600 rpm, so you don't have to spend a lot of time in the lower gears to get the most out of it. Not that the 250 won't rev, because it will. But above about 3000 rpm or so you're getting more noise than acceleration, and straining the innards, too.

The 3.55:1 rear axle ratio is obviously the right one for performance-minded drivers. In fact, if we bought a Camaro six without it on the collector's market, we'd immediately wire Chevrolet for the 3.55 gearset. Of course, the non-conformist can get even more by resorting to the hot rod crowd's usual—but not recommended—techniques: a 4.00:1 rear end, headers, and a hair-tune, for example. But that's not what the stock job was designed for. It was built to be an unbreakable, slow-revving engine with a long life. It was also vastly underrated in its time, probably because of the public's preoccupation with powerhouse V-8s. But as the medieval philosopher Roger Bacon said, "Great engines move slowly and are not so soon put out of frame."

A six-cylinder RS Camaro shouldn't be out at Lime Rock or Riverside anyway. The best place to enjoy it is on those twisty back roads, mixed with a bit of highway. The one road test we've seen of a six-cylinder model, conducted by *Motor Trend* magazine in 1968, summed things up very well: "The 250-cube 6 has enough torque to bowl over banana trees, and will even do a decent job on the highway scene. [It] represents a great little integrated driving package—a welcome relief from the power-mad supercar whose acceleration response is so intense and overwhelming that it takes on the character of a partially controlled ballistic missile . . . The machine is so well balanced . . . Not a wide-ovalled tire or a stiff suspension-that-feels-like-advanced-rigormortis-has-set-in anywhere, and the little machine fairly flys [sic] through the esses."

We found only two annoyances with this car, both of which could be corrected with the option book. The standard all-drum brake system was inadequate for anything except gentle, routine driving. We experienced early fade and rapidly rising pedal pressures on the first 80-mph panic stop. The convertible came with 11-inch front drums instead of the coupe's 9.5-inchers, but this wasn't enough. At the minimum, you needed the sintered metallic linings ($37.90) or, better yet, ventilated front discs ($79) with or without vacuum assist ($42.15). Power was also available for drum brake set-ups, but didn't do anything there except make them too pedal-sensitive.

Our other gripe was the manual steering—far too slow. (A 28:1 ratio was specified for the convertible, compared to 24:1 on coupes—also too slow.) But Chevy had a cure—a couple, in fact. You could order the regular power steering option ($84.30), which reduced the gearing to 17.5:1. There was also the short-spindle-arm N-44 quick-ratio steering, available with (15.6:1 ratio) or without (18:1) power assist ($15.80). Typically, Chevy had an option that could satisfy almost any owner's requirements.

We think the six-cylinder '67 Sport Coupe may be the thing for those enthusiasts who want an interesting, stylish collectible that can be treated as an everyday car. Aside from its limited rear seat room, this model still offers a practical combination of performance, economy, and dependability. And if you look at it as a substitute for a two-seat sports car, its cramped back seat actually becomes a plus. The 250-cid six is a fine engine, and complements the Camaro's many other well-known qualities. All in all, this car stands as one of the most versatile and enjoyable Chevrolets ever built.

SPECIFICATIONS

DIMENSIONS

Wheelbase: 108 inches. **Length:** 184.7 inches. **Width:** 72.3 inches. **Height:** 51.3 inches. **Weight:** 3025 pounds.

ENGINE

Type: ohv inline six. **Bore-and-Stroke:** 3.875×3.53 inches. **Displacement:** 250 cubic inches. **Bhp:** 155 @ 4200 rpm. **Torque:** 235 foot-pounds @ 1500 rpm.

TRANSMISSION

Four-speed all-synchromesh gearbox. **Gear ratios:** 3.11:1 (1st), 2.20:1 (2nd), 1.47:1 (3rd), 1.00:1 (4th). **Final drive ratio:** 3.55:1.

CHASSIS

Unitized body-chassis. **Front suspension:** independent with unequal-length A-arms, coil springs, tubular shocks. **Rear suspension:** live axle with semi-elliptic leaf springs and tubular shocks. **Brakes:** four-wheel drums, hydraulic, 168.9 square inches total swept area. **Steering:** recirculating ball gear, parallelogram linkage, 24:1 overall ratio, 4.3 turns lock-to-lock, 38.5 ft. turning circle.

PERFORMANCE

0-30 mph, seconds: 5.0
0-60 mph, seconds: 13.3
0-80 mph, seconds: 23.5
Standing-start quarter mile: 18.5 seconds @ 78 mph.
Speeds in gears (mph): 35 (1st), 62 (2nd), 80 (3rd), estimated 95 (4th).
Fuel consumption: 19-24 mpg, average 22.0

Birth of the Z-28: Wizards at Work

One of the best descriptions of the Camaro Z-28 came from an unlikely quarter back in April 1967. "When is a sports car not a sports car?" asked the Australian magazine *Sports Car World.* "If you answered 'when it's a yank tank' you could be wrong."

The editors went on to say that what Americans called sports cars—and this certainly included the Z-28—were not appreciated by enthusiasts "Down Under." This occurred "because we don't understand them . . . Australians still have a deep resentment of [cars like the Camaro] because our standard of living and car purchasing power hasn't yet permitted us to indulge in it . . . We hurt a lot of purists when we ran a funny test a few years back between the respective

Z-28 option was usually combined with RS gear, as on this '68.

Z-car buyers got more race-proven options in '68.

2-plus-2s of the variously distinguished houses of Ferrari and Pontiac. The big cumbersome Ponty went round a test track in the hands of an independent pilot as quick as the Ferrari . . . We're not saying a Pontiac *is* a Ferrari because they're designed for two infinitely different purposes and bred from far removed backgrounds. But we are bound to point out that *the American sporting machine is not the unsophisticated mechanical garbage can that most people would like to believe*" (Italics added).

The editors went on to note that their test Camaro (merely a 350 SS, not a Z-28) had "acceleration to match the best of Europe, braking of a high order, and handling that was surprisingly equal with some top Continental machinery on the faster bends." If a Camaro was slower on tight bends, well, you had to remember that twisty, crowded roads heavily influenced European auto engineering, while America is a land of wide-open spaces.

Finally, the editors declared, "Americans are probably more in contact with the world of sporting motoring than any other nationality in the world: after all they own half the world's sports cars, and they are the export territory for about 90 percent of those very cars produced on the Continent. If you want to get really basic you'll have to realize that America is probably the only reason half those European concessionaires [manufacturers] are in business!" Blunt words—and from the British Commonwealth at that.

The Z-28 was precisely the kind of car these perceptive Aussies were talking about. By European standards it did not seem like much. It was not an exotic, hand-built *gran turismo* with sophisticated engineering and built at the rate of one or ten a day. Instead, it was a conventional design based on mass-produced components right off the GM parts shelf. The genius of the car—or rather its designers—was that all its seemingly ordinary pieces worked so impressively well together. This is why the Z-28 (originally the designation was just another of the

Deep chin spoiler and cold-air hood marked the 1969 Z-28.

Mark Donohue turned Z into a winner by seat-of-the-pants testing.

company's Regular Production Option codes) became what Michael Lamm termed a "Legend in its Own Time." It was truly magical.

If you can credit one man with the Z-28 concept, it would certainly be Vincent W. Piggins, who had been a Chevrolet engineer since 1956. "After Ford released the Mustang," Piggins said,* "they had about two years on us before Chevrolet could get the Camaro into the 1967 product line. I felt in my activity, which deals with product promotion and how to get the most promotional mileage from a car from the performance standpoint, that we needed to develop a performance image for the Camaro that would be superior to the Mustang's.

"Along comes SCCA in creating the Trans-Am sedan racing class for professional drivers in 1966, aimed for the 1967 season. I made it a point to have several discussions with SCCA officials—notably Jim Kaser, John Bishop and Tracy Byrd—and one thing led to another. I suggested a vehicle that would fit this class and, I believe—supported by what Chevrolet might do with the Camaro—it gave them the heart to push ahead and make up the rules, regulations and so forth for the Trans-Am series. I feel this was really the creation of the Trans-Am as we know it."

As originally devised, the Trans-Am series had two classes. The one we're concerned with here applied to "sedans" with a 116-inch wheelbase or less, and engine displacement not exceeding 305 cubic inches. The Camaro had a rear seat, so it qualified as a "sedan."

The rules also provided that, to be eligible, a car had to be produced in quantities of at least 1000 units in any model year. Though Chevrolet sold only 602 of the 1967-model Z-28s, it met the minimum production requirement by homologating the standard 350-cid Camaro under *Federación International d'Automobile* (FIA) Group I rules, then qualifying the car with the Z-28 *option* under Group II. Clever.

The original plot for the Z-28, according to Piggins, was to combine the following components in one package: F-41 heavy-duty suspension, front disc brakes, metallic-lined rear drum brakes, the 24:1 quick-ratio steering gear, Corvette 15×6 wheels with 7.75×15 tires, and a special hood with functional air intake. Together, these made a stock Camaro into a Z-28. The drivetrain would have comprised GM's close-ratio four-speed manual transmission and the 283-cid V-8. But here, Piggins had a "better idea."

"While we were driving the [prototype], I mentioned that we'd put the 283 into it because we'd built that size engine before. But I suggested that it might be a lot

* Quotations are used by permission of interviewer Michael Lamm, *op. cit.*

A peek under the '69 hood. Dual Holley carbs were a $500 option.

better to take the 327 block and put the 283 crank into it, giving us 4×3 bore and stroke. That would put displacement at 302.4 cid, just under the SCCA's 305 limit. So [Chevrolet general manager Elliot M. "Pete"] Estes immediately agreed, especially being an engineer and knowing the potential this car could have."

Chevrolet rated the 302's output at a very conservative 290 brake horsepower, with 290 foot-pounds of torque. This, as one magazine put it, was "laughable . . . Four hundred comes much nearer the truth. This is a fistful of energy any way you dissect it. A 4-inch bore allows generously large valves, and the short 3-inch stroke keeps friction low and lets this engine wind to 7200 without missing a beat." Complementing the 283 crank in the 327 block was a huge, four-barrel Holley carburetor on a special oversize manifold with large ports and valves, along with a 346-degree-duration high-lift cam and cast-iron headers. All of this was the very heart of the Z-28's motive power—and tremendous it was.

People who wanted a Z-28 in the early days—and they *did* want them, in larger numbers than Chevy expected—could have the most basic set-up for about $3800. The Z-28 option itself (302 V-8, F-41 suspension, quick steering, special trim, and Rally wheels with wide-tread GT tires) added only about $400 to the under-$3000 base price of a plain-Jane Camaro coupe. But to get this hot package you *also* had to order front disc brakes with power assist and one of three available four-speed manual transmissions. This boosted the price by another $300-400.

And that was for the "economy special." You couldn't buy a Z-28 in convertible form, but there was an impressive array of other extra-cost items to tempt you: the Rally Sport package, Positraction, sintered-metallic rear brake drum linings, headers, ram-air system, fiberglass rear spoiler. The most expensive option, offered for 1968-69, was a pair of 600-cfm four-barrel Holley carburetors mounted on a special manifold—$500, plus dealer installation.

So, it wasn't impossible to work a Z-28 up to the $5000 level. Even so, this was not considered outlandish by those interested in winning races, though it did turn off a few would-be owners of the street machines.

Winning races was, of course, Chevy's primary aim in developing the Z-28. The first 25 cars were built before mid-January 1967 (contrary to some rumors, the Z-28 was *not* a "1967½" introduction). Most were sent to dealerships with an active involvement in racing, such as the Don Yenko and Roger Penske outlets in Pennsylvania, Nickey Chevrolet in Chicago, and Ron Tonkin in Portland, Oregon. Most of these dealers began preparing and entering the cars in Trans-Am competition. In due course the exercise paid off: Camaro was champion in the over-2-liter class for both 1968 and '69. And this meant—to Chevrolet's

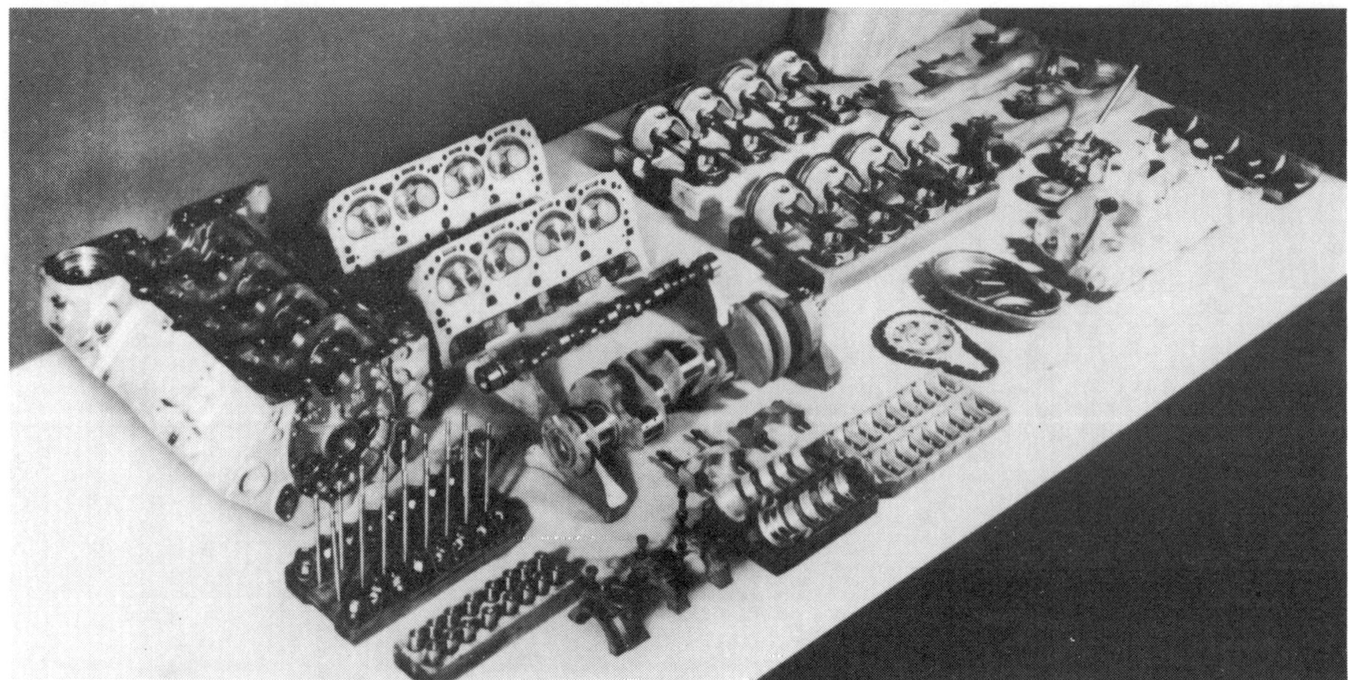

Laid out for inspection: the Z-28's muscular 302 V-8.

unmitigated delight—that Mustang wasn't.

Though many driver/dealer duos drove to success with the Z-28, the twosome that stood out most was that of Mark Donohue and Roger Penske. Penske, a prominent Pennsylvania Chevy agent with several dealerships, was a fine racing driver in his own right, and had known Donohue since their early SCCA days. Roger asked Mark to drive a Camaro for him in the 1967 Trans-Am campaign. Due to what must have been a misunderstanding, Donohue was asked to spec-out the suspension, which he didn't know a thing about. (The engine prep, by Traco of California, was beyond criticism; its engines just wouldn't stop.) Due to Donohue's inexperience, the team's initial appearances at Daytona and Sebring were marred by handling woes. What's more, the cars didn't brake well. Donohue eked out a second-in-class at Sebring, but the win was Mustang's.

'69 hood scoop pulled air from high-turbulence area at rear of hood.

At this point Chevrolet Research & Development stepped in, determined to make the Z-28 a winner. The braking problem was solved by reversing the lines from their stock position, allowing the master cylinder's larger piston to work the front discs rather than the rear drums. But the Penske car still did not do well in its next two outings, so Chevrolet invited Donohue and car to the Milford, Michigan proving grounds for a thorough going over.

There, the Camaro went through a tremendous number of tests, many made with sophisticated sensors attached to the suspension, drivetrain and body. Computer analysis then helped the engineers zero-in on the weak points. Two things were learned: first, the body needed strengthening to prevent flex that was interfering with suspension geometry; second, the right rear traction bar also upset suspension geometry (it was later removed).

Remaining suspension problems were thrashed out in practice before the next event at Upper Marlboro, Maryland. Chevrolet R&D sent a discreetly marked van—with Pennsylvania license plates—loaded with enough spare parts, tools and equipment to handle any possible need. Various suspension changes were made, then Donohue would test each one out on the track. After an exhausting number of trial-and-error evaluations, followed by a complete pre-race teardown, the Penske Z-28 was at last ready. The work paid off: Camaro scored its first victory in Trans-Am competition, with a 63-mph average. That wouldn't sound like much unless you'd driven the narrow, twisty Marlboro course. It was an impressive win alright, and Donohue began to smile again.

But by now, there wasn't much time left for the Z-28 to recover the 1967 series, and the loss of the number-one machine in a road accident before a California race cost more time while a back-up car was keyed-in. Still, Donohue won the last two races of the season, a portent of things to come.

During preparation for the 1968 battles, the Z-28 racing program began to take on an other-worldly aspect. If Ford folk could have looked in on it, they might have been discouraged—and impressed—by the amount of technology being mustered by their rich and determined rivals. While the Penske team developed its '68 cars based on seat-of-the-pants experiences from the year before, GM was at work on some far-out engineering: independent rear suspension, four-wheel disc brakes, quick-release (by engine vacuum) disc pads to speed up pit stops. Of these, only the irs was discarded because its effect on the Camaro's actual track performance was negligible. And as if that weren't enough, Chevy came up with something that could actually monitor the car *while it was being raced.* It wouldn't have looked out of place in "Star Wars" years later: a "telemetry van," loaded with computers. These were hooked into radio-telephone links with the car, and recorded every physical action/reaction that went on throughout the race.

The "telemetry van" was an imaginative stroke which proved crucial to the 1968 racing effort. With the data it supplied, engineers constructed computer models of the car; then, by tinkering with suspension, brakes and other components, they could design—again by computer—an optimum mechanical and handling package to fit any race course. You could almost stage a protest under the banner "Unfair to Mustang," if you were sure Ford wasn't working on something similar—and nobody *was* sure, of course.

The kick-off event for the '68 Trans-Am series was at Daytona, but again proved a disappointment. Camaro finished second-in-class due to cracked heads and time lost in subsequent pit stops. At Sebring, though, Penske and GM couldn't have asked for more. The two team cars finished third and fourth overall, trailing only a pair of 911 Porsches, and took the GT class one-two. After that, Camaro virtually romped through the rest of the year, winning nine of the remaining 11 races to capture the over-2-liter crown.

The following year—after considerable work with the "telemetry van"—there were two new Penske cars, and it was a repeat story: eight out of 12 Trans-Am events won by Camaro, which held the title for the second straight year. Mustang had been defeated.

However, 1970 was a gloomy year for Z-fans. Penske and Donohue were spirited away by American Motors, and were soon setting records with Javelins. The new, second-generation Camaro didn't go on sale until the season was well under way, and by then it was too late for anyone to do much with it, even someone with Donohue's kind of skill and persistence. But the Z-28 had made its point. Thanks to the incredible devotion of Penske, Donohue and Chevrolet R&D, it had become, in just two short years, a performance legend.

Changes in the Z-28's specifications for 1968 and '69 were slight but important, and are worth setting down for the record. For 1968, the engine stayed basically the same, but crankshaft bearing diameters were enlarged, and the special dual four-barrel manifold ($500 plus dealer installation) appeared. Four-wheel disc brakes, giving a total swept lining area of 461.2 square inches, were offered as a "service option" late in the model year. Quick steering (21.4:1 ratio) became standard, and an even quicker ratio (17.9:1) was available at extra cost. Comparable gearing was on hand for power assist. There was a longer list of competition options too, including special steering components, plastic racing bucket seats, air dams and rear spoilers. Another useful goody was a double-thick front anti-sway bar to replace the standard item. Five-leaf rear springs with heavy-duty staggered shocks became standard Z-28 wear, and that tricky righthand radius rod was deleted.

The production '69 model, last of the first-generation cars, was distinguished by the addition of a "cold-air" hood, featuring a rear-facing scoop angled to catch the wind at a point of maximum turbulence. The 302 V-8 was switched to four-bolt mains, and the 15-inch Rally wheels were slimmed down from 7 to 6 inches in width. In place of the standard Goodyear tires came Firestone

E70-15 Sports Car 200s. Finally, the four-wheel disc brakes became a Regular Production Option for '69 instead of a "service option" (which meant you found a few of them on the street, but not many).

In production, the 1969 model is the all-time Z-28 leader: 19,014 were built, against 7199 of the '68 version and 602 of the '67s. The next best year is 1977, when 14,349 copies of a much detuned and considerably tamer Z-28 were built. The ponycar craze had peaked by 1969. It then plummeted in the early '70s, bottoming out with the oil crisis of 1973-74. Although some later Z-28s sold briskly, it was '69 that saw the model at its peak.

How fast was the Z-28, really? Well, Smokey Yunick took his own car to Bonneville in October 1967, after having been denied entry to the final Trans-Am race. His drivers included Mickey Thompson, Curtis Turner and Bunkie Blackburn. Thompson managed a flying mile at 174.344 mph, beating the Class C American Stock record set in 1963 (by a Studebaker GT Hawk) by almost 30 mph. Yunick managed to blow his engine in the standing 10-kilometer runs, but after he put it back together he broke another record by running for 12 hours straight at over 140 mph. All told, Yunick's Z-28 shattered 259 Class B, Class C, and Unlimited world speed records. (The Class B runs were made with the same car powered by an L-78 396 V-8, which gave a top speed of 183.486 mph—beating a record set by Pontiac in 1962.)

Street Zs, of course, were not tuned to this level, but they were pretty impressive nonetheless. (See the following driving impression.) *Car and Driver* magazine tested one with the hairy, twin four-barrel set-up, recording 0-60 mph in 5.3 seconds, and a stunning quarter-mile time of 13.77 seconds at 107.39 mph—real drag race stuff. Of course, they also had the advantage of having Sam Posey to do the driving.

No matter how you look at it—street, drag race, Trans-Am or Salt Flats—the Z-28 was a tremendous high-performance machine. It remains so to this day, especially after the so-called performance cars of the sickly '70s, which reflected, perhaps, the nation's changing concerns. The fact is there will probably never again be such a rip-snorting, fire-breathing, hairy-chested grand tourer as this. The Z-28s that survive into the energy-conscious '80s have long since become collector's prizes—artifacts of a memorable age that now seems long ago and far away.

Penske and Donohue switched to Javelin for 1970 Trans-Am season. Camaro didn't do well that year.

Camaro

Color Gallery I

1967 Sport Coupe

1967 Sport Coupe

1967 SS-350 Convertible

1967 RS Coupe

1967 SS-350 Coupe

1967 Sport Coupe

1968 Sport Coupe

1969 Sport Coupe

1969 Penske/Donohue Z-28

1969 Z-28 (Owner: Greg Shingler)

1969 Z-28 (Owner: Greg Shingler)

1970 SS

1970 Rally Sport

1972 Rally Sport

1972 Sport Coupe (Owner: Ray Dunn)

Driving Impressions: 1969 Z-28

Chevrolet general manager "Pete" Estes was bullish about the '69 Camaro Z-28. "We only planned on selling about 400 in 1968," he said, "but instead, we had 7000 orders. Boy, there are kids out there, and they have money. And when they hear how Mark Donohue cleans up in Trans-Am with a Z-28, they've just *got* to have one for themselves. In 1969, we plan to sell 27,000. Can you imagine? 27,000!"

Well, only about 19,000 of the '69 Z-28s were sold, but that was still the record for the model. Small wonder: the '69 was the very essence of the whole Z-28 idea.

Small but significant styling changes occured on all Camaros that year. While the 1967-68 car was smooth and clean, the '69 was bulkier and more aggressive. A no-nonsense eggcrate grille, vee'd out in the middle, combined with crisp, creased "eyebrows" over the wheel openings and pressed-in hashmarks ahead of the rear wheels to suggest purpose and performance. On Z-28s, such as Greg Shingler's impressive silver example shown here, this more extroverted look is carried to its logical conclusion. A big air dam rides under the wide-mouth grille. A huge cold-air intake sweeps back from the front of the hood, which is adorned with broad racing stripes. Chrome Rally wheels and wide tires (Goodyear GTs are used here;

The '69 Z-28 in its element: at speed through a fast open-road sweeper.

'69 Z sported all the performance touches of the day, including decklid spoiler and fat tires.

Chin spoiler was a new item for '69, as was mean-looking cold-air hood.

Firestone SC-200s were original) add to the image. Two more stripes ride the rear deck, which is capped by a prominent spoiler. The '69 Z-car looks—and is—mean, hairy, rugged, and ready to eat just about any Mustang for lunch. While other sporty cars followed the trend toward comfort and compromise in 1969, the Z-28 became even more of a hot-blooded thoroughbred—a racing car suitable for occasional use on the street. Back then, a lot of people were surprised the beast was actually legal.

The engine, which makes all the noise in this rig (and a lot of it), idles at 900 rpm—lumpily and uneasily to be sure (it would rather be winding up to 4000-plus). It's ideally designed for a dual-purpose machine—debored 327 block with a strong forged-steel crankshaft related to (but not the same as) the standard cast-iron crank in the 283. Standard tune gives what we estimate to be 60 bhp more than Chevy's rated 290, thanks to a hot 346-degree-duration camshaft, with 118 degrees of overlap. Compression ratio is 11:1, so the highest octane gas is mandatory. In these days of low-calorie unleaded, you either have to fill a Z-28 at the local airport, or carry cans of octane additive. If you do the latter, carry *several* cans: the typical mileage ranges between 8 and 14 mpg, and averages about 12.5.

Some aspects of the '69 interior aren't as nice as on the 1967-68 models. You notice these as soon as you swing behind the wheel. Headrests, dictated by that year's safety regulations, tend to obstruct over-the-shoulder vision; however, they're removable. The redesigned dash dispenses with the original, simple twin-dial layout and substitutes a slightly curved arrangement with round instruments in square housings. This concoction, by Don Schwartz's interior studio at GM Styling, may have been prompted by the arrival of flow-through ventilation the year before, although the air vents were first incorporated without changing the original dash design. We liked the two-spoke '69 steering wheel, but found the instruments hard to read. The auxiliary gauges, again carried ahead of the shifter atop the plastic console, are even harder to spot, especially when conducting the Z-28 in what it does best.

Motor Trend magazine drove a Z-car with the optional dual four-barrel Holley carburetors (the car pictured has the standard four-barrel set-up). A couple of *MT*'s impressions are worth repeating. "Wild as it may have been for 1968—eliciting comments like, 'Man, sounds great!' just while idling at a stoplight—it has become downright immoral for 1969 . . . The cam rocks the Z-28 and furls brows of adjacent motorists."

A touch of the accelerator—and it had better *be* a touch because of the hair-trigger throttle linkage—is all that's necessary to launch this projectile. The standard four-barrel induction system delivers 0-60 mph times in the low-7s or high-6s (against a startling 5.5 seconds or so with the twin Holleys and headers). The standing-start quarter-mile time is under 15 seconds, and results in over 100 mph. To produce these figures, the drill is to rev it to 3500 rpm, then pop the clutch. Our lack of nerve (or is it common sense?) has kept us from seeing a Z-28 to its maximum velocity in the past, so our top speed figure here is estimated from contemporary road tests. It should be pointed out that with a numerically lower axle ratio the '69 Z-28 was capable of close to 150 mph flat out. That sort of thing is pretty academic these days, and besides, the speedo only reads to 120 mph. But it was fun when gas was a quarter-a-gallon.

One of the Z-28's drawbacks (and not unexpected in a semi-competition machine designed for high revs) is anemic low-end response. Torque peaks at a lofty 4200 rpm, and very little happens below that, which is why you have to rev it so high to get under way. If we owned this car, we would make regular pilgrimmages to Nevada, which still has a few places where you can run indecently—if not legally—fast, say at 100-plus. That's Z-28 country for sure.

Manipulating the close-ratio gearbox is pleasant. Shifts are fast and clean, and the synchromesh is literally unbeatable. With all this power underfoot you

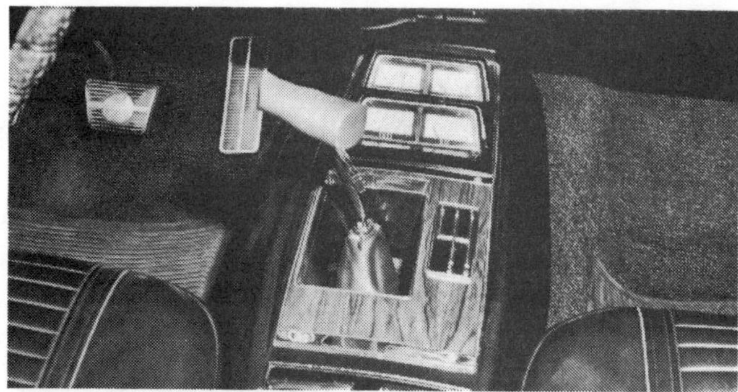

Console isn't the best place for the minor dials.

"Astro Ventilation" included adjustable dash vents.

'69 interior looks–and is–all business.

Main gauge cluster houses speedo, tach, and clock.

Chin spoiler helped high-speed stability but left scant ground clearance.

Cold-air duct was really a rear-facing scoop.

Air cleaner gasket mated to inside of hood.

need every one of those gears too, even though you can easily exceed the Federal limit in first. (In 1968, *Car Life* magazine noted that the Z-28 was one machine that needed its four forward gears. In most cars of its type, said the writer, torque peaked too far down the scale to make four speeds really necessary. But the Z had all kinds of muscle available, and was eager to spin over that 4000-rpm mark.)

Clutch pressure is surprisingly light. Chevrolet deserves credit here, for this is a hefty, 11-inch-diameter clutch with spring pressures over 2700 pounds—larger and stronger even than the one used with the 396 V-8. Yet anyone can manage the Z-28's clutch, most without stomping very hard on the pedal.

When it comes to handling, the Z-28 is definitely tighter and more grippy than the standard 1969 Camaro, although the suspension specs are not all that different. The Z's front spring rates are the same as those of the 327-equipped models, while the rear rates are higher by approximately 125 percent than on the 396 versions. Naturally, all the big-engined Camaros used multi-leaf, instead of single-leaf, rear springs. There would be no way to keep the back end on the ground with the standard set-up.

Our general impression of this Camaro on the road was one of harshness. It's a competition machine first, and a road car a *very* distant second. This shows from the moment you turn the key. The ride is probably too stiff for the average driver. Behind the wheel, you're constantly aware that this is a Detroit car, not a European one. The high beltline, low seating position and enveloping dash create a "sitting-in-a-bathtub" feeling; the hood looks enormous. And after all, this *is* a big car, especially by 1981 standards. There's a lot of mass to fling around at any speed, let alone the esoteric velocities this car can achieve. These factors, combined with the poor gas mileage, raucous engine and weak low-rpm response, make the '69 Z-28 very much a special-purpose car.

That said, the Z's performance at really high speeds is something to stir the blood. *Road & Track* magazine perhaps put it best in its original test of a '68 model: "With its wide tires the Z-28 is a stable, near-neutral car that has no trouble setting excellent lap times

Peaky 302 V-8 demands lots of revs to get the Z-28 launched.

around any reasonably smooth course. The trick with a car like this, with all that torque available in the right gear, is to find that point where you're using just enough throttle to get it around a turn neutrally rather than plowing or spinning out." Once you've done that, you will enjoy yourself.

We found braking fairly good in all but really punishing use, when fade set in after the second or third stop. The trouble is, severe use can be commonplace given the tremendous performance—at least it probably was when cars like the Z-28 were driven daily instead of just to the occasional meet or competition.

SPECIFICATIONS

DIMENSIONS

Wheelbase: 108 inches. **Length:** 184.6 inches. **Width:** 72.3 inches. **Height:** 50.9 inches. **Weight:** 3300 pounds.

ENGINE

Type: ohv 90-degree V-8. **Bore-and-Stroke:** 4.00 × 3.00 inches. **Displacement:** 302 cubic inches. **Estimated bhp:** 350 @ 5300 rpm. **Estimated torque:** 325 foot-pounds @ 4200 rpm.

CHASSIS

Unitized body/chassis. **Front suspension:** independent with unequal-length A-arms, coil springs, tubular shocks and anti-roll bar. **Rear suspension:** live axle with semi-elliptic leaf springs and tubular shocks. **Brakes:** disc front, drums rear, 332 square inches total swept area. **Steering:** integral-assist recirculating ball gear, parallelogram linkage, 17:1 overall ratio, 2.8 turns lock-to-lock, 36.5 ft. turning circle.

PERFORMANCE

0-30 mph, seconds: 3.5
0-60 mph, seconds: 7.2
0-80 mph, seconds: 10.3
Standing-start quarter mile: 14.8 seconds @ 103 mph.
Speeds in gears (mph): 63 (1st), 87 (2nd), 115 (3rd), estimated 135 (4th).
Fuel consumption: 8-14 mpg, average 12.5.

Chevy chief engineer Alex Mair (left) with then general manager "Pete" Estes in the late '60s.

It's easy to understand why brake problems troubled the Trans-Am team from time to time, and why GM had to come up with four-wheel discs as a service option.

How does the '69 Z-car compare to its arch-rival, the Shelby-Mustang GT-350? We won't get into outright performance—there are too many variables. But we think the Camaro is somewhat more comfortable. Actually, there's not much to choose in this area between the two, although comfort has usually been ignored in evaluating cars like this in the past. Certainly with the performance of a GT-350 or Z-28 you want to be reasonably well catered to. The driving position in the Camaro seemed more relaxed, and there was more room behind the wheel than in the Shelby. That includes lots of elbow room for the arm-flinging required to careen at 90-plus through corners marked "45 mph." And you do that a lot in a Z-28. Honest you do.

Never again will one car offer as much brute performance for the money.

Second Generation: The Mitchell Legacy

The second-generation Camaro appeared in 1970. Remarkably, it was still in production over 11 years later—and in basically the same form. It was predominately a designer's car. There were fast ones, of course, as we shall see. But a double-barreled assault from Federal regulations and a changing market made the 1970-81 Camaros considerably tamer than their hell-bent-for-leather predecessors. Styling, not performance, is what has made the post-1969 generation a classic in its own time. And, though many people were responsible for its smooth good looks, all the final decisions were made by just one individual: William L. Mitchell.

Probably more than anyone else in Detroit, Bill Mitchell has influenced the way cars look today—even those that are not General Motors products. In fact, it's fair to say that Mitchell indirectly contributed to the lines of cars like the Ford Granada and Chrysler Cordoba—perhaps more than Dearborn or Highland Park would be willing to admit. Over the years, both competitors have tried to one-up GM Styling and the gospel according to Mitchell. Sometimes they succeeded, but many times they did not.

Theodore MacManus once said of Cadillac, "If the leader leads, he remains the leader." GM has set the trends for Detroit styling for some 20 years now. MacManus also said that leaders have their detractors. Bill Mitchell has certainly had his share. A few of them were other designers, some of them also-rans in a profession he dominated for 20 years and influenced for 40. Others were second-guessers from outside the auto industry. Based on the chrome-covered American glitter wagons they saw, they concluded that no Detroit stylist was worth a dime. But being a fair critic requires thorough knowledge of an individual designer and his work, plus an appreciation for the enormous pressure automotive stylists feel from sales people and higher management.

Then there were those who simply didn't like Bill Mitchell's style. "His round body clad in bright scarlet or mylar chrome-coated leathers, astride one of his adolescent fantasy motorcycles, is enough to force a guffaw from Samuel Beckett," one English reviewer put it. Rubbish, to use an appropriate English expression. Bill Mitchell's choice in dress or personal transportation had no bearing on his professional competence, which was obvious and considerable.

When Mitchell relieved Harley Earl as chief of GM Design in 1958, he stepped into a pair of rather large shoes—shoes some said were too large for anyone to fill. But fill them he did, usually by supplying just what the automobile buyer wanted most. The English writer continued, "If vulgarity was called for, supreme vulgarity was forthcoming." It should also be said that when elegance and strength of line were called for, Mitchell responded—and generously. Like other automobile companies, GM Styling has had its ugly periods, and GM has built ugly cars. However, the cars from the Mitchell years—the second-generation Camaro prominent among them—have, by and large, been fresh and exciting, often radical, and rarely uninteresting.

Bill Mitchell retired a few years ago. This means that the third-generation 1982 Camaro will be less expressive of his ideas than the 1970-81 design. We'll just have to wait to see whether it will stand the test of time as well.

During a conversation with Mitchell, it was suggested that the second-generation Camaro and the 1965-69 Corvair were his two best creations. Mitchell agreed. "The first [1967-69 Camaros] were done too fast, we didn't get a chance to do much. But the second-series cars have been in production for over a decade now, and they're selling better than ever . . . Stirling Moss saw the first one and he said, 'Bill, you've really got a classic. The detail, it's not all carved up, it's got a nice sweep.' It's been very popular in Europe, too."

The critical difference that shaped the "1970½" Camaro was the decision that it be a ground-up design. There would be none of the compromises forced on the 1967-69 series, such as a cowl shared with the Nova. "Mitchell had convinced management that the Camaro could stand on its own feet," says one former GM stylist, "that it could be profitable enough to qualify the expense necessary in creating its own unique body dies. Of course, many of the body parts were shared by the Pontiac Firebird." (The Firebird would remain basically a Camaro clone. Even so, certain items, notably the door panels, would not be interchangeable.)

The important thing is that unlike the original, the second Camaro design evolved the way it did because the car no longer had to share body parts with a sedan. This gave stylists an unprecedented amount of freedom, tempered by the increasing number of government standards which often seemed to stifle creativity.

Ferrari is favorite of many GM designers, as this September 1967 comparison shows.

First clays picked up where '69 left off.

Notchback roofline was only briefly considered.

Mitchell vetoed this simple loop grille for a more "important-looking" face.

What emerged was a shape that could be (and was) successfully updated to meet regulations as they took effect, but without the kind of measures that messed up many other cars of the '70s. For instance, the soft-nose facelift for 1978 made the second-series Camaro look better than ever.

Irv Rybicki, now GM vice-president for design and Mitchell's successor, remembered the evolution of the 1970½ Camaro in an interview with Michael Lamm*. "We started planning [it] immediately after the first project ended. That second car, as I remember, wasn't developed in the studios per se. We initially sat down in what we call the body development room, where we package our vehicles, and we worked very closely with Jack Humbert and Dave Holls; we were in there with [body engineer] Vince Kaptur and we worked every day to get the seat placed just right, the rockers where we wanted them, the cowl at a certain point, always

---

**Rybicki interview excerpted from* The Great Camaro *by Michael Lamm with permission of the author.*

Both Kamm-type and smooth rear ends were in the running for 1970.

Stylists again pushed for a sport-wagon. Hidden windshield pillar was Hank Haga's idea.

Wagon might have made it had Firebird shared Camaro's door panels.

with the mental picture of the silhouette we were after.

"We moved the elements around until we had the package that looked like it would present the kind of body shape we were after—a little shoulder on the car, the wheels right out with the skin, the proper height . . . I always say to the creative staff in our building that if we can get the anatomy, the shape of the skin is easy. The key to the appearance of a car is in its structure, in its anatomy: where you place the seats, how high, how wide, its length, the correct tumblehome, the proper relationship of the wheels to the sheetmetal. If you've got those elements, you're going to get an automobile that's very appealing to the eye, and that's the way this one was."

The second generation was developed strictly as a coupe. A convertible was never even considered, though a wagon might have come along had there been full body panel interchangeability between Camaro and Firebird. The decision to abandon the convertible came about for two reasons. For one thing, tooling costs would have been considerable because the new F-body would be unrelated to any sedan. This meant that tooling had to be paid for with a much lower production volume, too low to justify a second body style. Also, convertibles had faded in popularity by the end of the '60s, so potential sales did not justify the expense, either. The advent of air conditioning and efficient flow-through ventilation systems had contributed to the ragtop's decline. There was also a fear at the time (false, as it turned out later) that the National Highway Traffic Safety Administration (NHTSA) was about to enact standards for rollover protection. These standards would have effectively banned the sale of full convertibles in the U.S. (Many companies used this as an excuse to drop their open models, but the main reasons were marginal sales and low profitability, not the threat of government regulation.)

Once again, the styling brief was placed in the competent hands of Henry Haga. Again, the GM styling hierarchy (including Holls, Rybicki and Chuck Jordan) observed and directed. Bill Mitchell was still the final authority. But this time, styling compromises were repeatedly shot down. At one point, Rybicki noted, engineers insisted on a higher cowl line than the stylists wanted, so components like heater, radio, glovebox, instrument panel—not to mention the option-

Jaguar XJ inspired 1970 frontispiece.

Compare this with similar view of production car pg. 55.

Interim semi-fastback style went through several stages between late 1967 and early '68.

Designers also played with a "landau" type roof. Fortunately, it wasn't adopted.

al air conditioner—would fit. "Hank brought this to my attention, so I met with the engineers" said Rybicki. "But they wouldn't budge. They wanted more space . . . I called in Bill Mitchell. Bill quickly resolved the situation in a meeting by telling the engineers that a low silhouette was critical to the sporty character of this car, and that we absolutely weren't going to raise the cowl even a fraction of an inch." And that was *that.*

Was the new model's clean, graceful fastback shape part of the formula from the first? Not really, but it arrived early. Haga and his staff considered many proposals, including notchbacks and semi-fastbacks, with both smoothly rounded and cut-off Kamm-type tails. Some of the initial clay models, done as early as 1966, were reminiscent of the 1968 and later Corvettes. But the near-timeless form that would become familiar to Camaro enthusiasts was simply the one that looked best. And it was never challenged by any committee.

Probably the only serious question about the side elevation was in the greenhouse area: should it have rear quarter windows or not? A variety of treatments was tried. The final solution was to use very long doors and no quarter windows. A few people complained

Rear side windows proved a stumbling block. Ultimately, they were eliminated.

Very late clay bears "Berlinetta" script. Note rounded upper door glass corners.

By late '67, Camaro project was coded "Prova 70."

Another semi-fastback from early 1968.

A definite Aston-Martin influence is evident here.

Squared "mouth" won management's favor early.

This variation was probably intended for RS model.

Thin horizontal bars were tried for grille cavity.

about the size and weight of those doors, but the styling effect was clean and striking. The decision was primarily a matter of cost, according to GM designers. Eliminating that extra piece of glass and its associated hardware freed up money that could be used in other areas of the car—and it certainly didn't hurt the looks.

Front and rear treatments were argued over much longer than the side elevation. Performance-minded stylists wanted a high, aggressive tail with a prominent spoiler, as on the first-generation Z-28s. They didn't get it. What prevailed was a smooth, low tail with a semi-Kamm-style flat panel. (The Firebird, which was developing at the same time, got a more complex double panel to hide the fact—literally—that its inner trunk wall was shared with Camaro.) Up front, early clays proposed a rather common-looking loop-style bumper surrounding a horizontal-bar grille *cum* headlights. This was scratched in favor of a much more "important-looking" square grille and dual, rather than quad, headlights. The latter choice marked a trend away from the quad set-ups that had been so prevalent in the industry since the late '50s.

Between headlights and grille, RS models carried smaller round parking lights—a direct crib from the Jaguar XJ sedan, a design which had many admirers at GM. An eggcrate grille texture was used to "enrich" the front end far beyond what was normally expected in the car's price class. Instead of a conventional American "face," the new Camaro wore a grille that looked much like those of some very expensive European grand touring cars, notably Ferrari. This helped its lines enormously, especially compared to the clumsier, more Detroit-style split grille adopted for the new Firebird.

The interior was carefully laid out in Don Schwarz' studio, again largely by George Angersbach. Irv Rybicki remains enthusiastic about this aspect of the design: "A lot of time on the interior was spent on 'human engineering.' We were aiming at something that was close to the Corvette in terms of ride and handling and ease of operation. This had to be a driver's car, with the shift lever correctly placed relative to the steering wheel; all the controls just right.

"For example, if you sit in a Camaro with your hands on the steering wheel, after the seat is properly adjusted, let your right hand drop off the wheel. It simply falls on the shift knob. The door latch is right where it should be. Every control is equally well placed. The interior is a very good job of human engineering."

With all due respect to Mr. Rybicki, it could be argued that "human engineering" should have been carried further. For instance, the pedals ended up too far forward, requiring long-legged drivers to snug the seat too far up for a comfortable reach to the steering wheel. The wheel itself had a wide horizontal bar which hid the heater controls, turn signal indicator lights, and ashtray from the driver's sight. The ashtray, in turn, was sited so that when it was pulled out the driver's knee could bang against it. The instruments were well placed, though, with speedometer and fuel gauge or

Early interior sketch shows designers' concern with proper gauge placement.

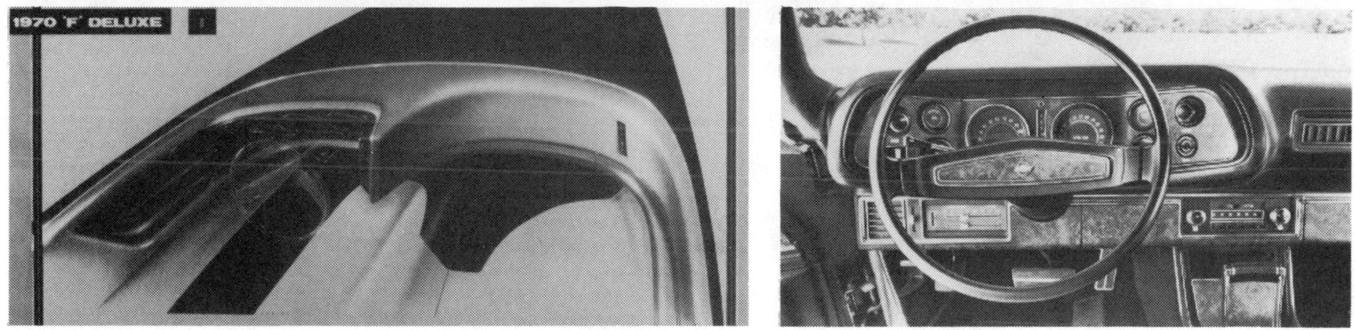

Curved dash was contemplated early on (left), led to concave oval on production cars (right).

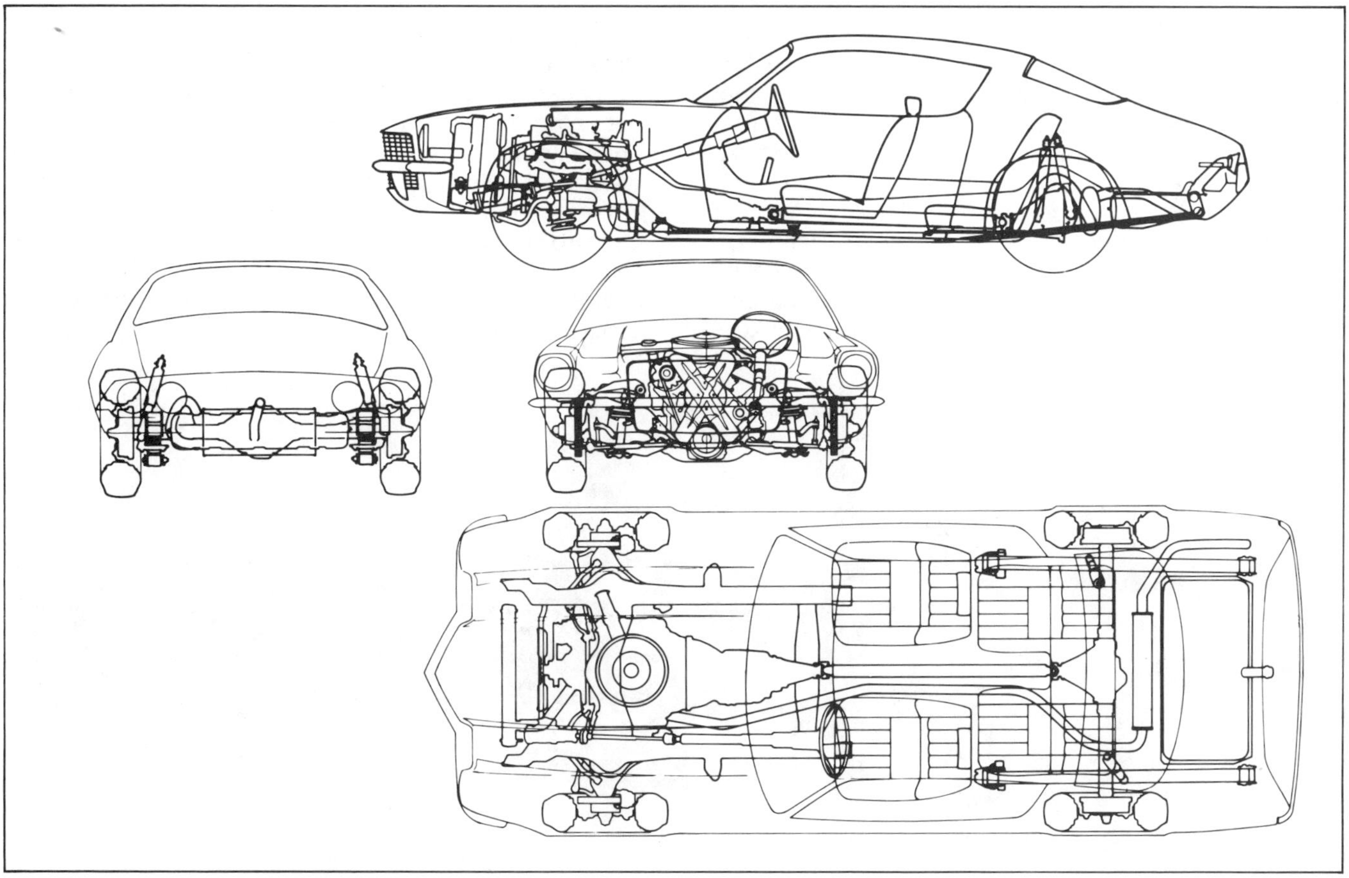

Second generation continued with unit body and front sub-frame. Suspension was thoroughly revised.

1970 RS had split bumper, Endura-covered grille frame.

Standard grille was bisected by bumper.

1970 "Landau" show car was built for singer Glen Campbell.

optional tach squarely in the middle. But the tach's "redline" extended from 6500 to 8000 rpm, leaving the driver to wonder exactly what the limit was. Finally, Federal regulations dictated that the ignition key could not be removed from the column lock without first putting the car in reverse—annoying.

The instrument panel bears mention here because it survived unchanged through the 1978 models. Angersbach's design was a variation on the curved panels pioneered in the early '60s by Pontiac and Studebaker. Unlike these, however, the curved portion of the Camaro's panel did not house the heater controls (mounted below and to the left) or radio (lower right). These items, along with the light and wiper switches, were somewhat awkward to reach.

The general engineering concept of the original Camaro continued on its replacement: unit body/chassis with front sub-frame, a similar lineup of engines, standard front disc brakes. But there was a subtle "deemphasis of performance," as *Sports Car*

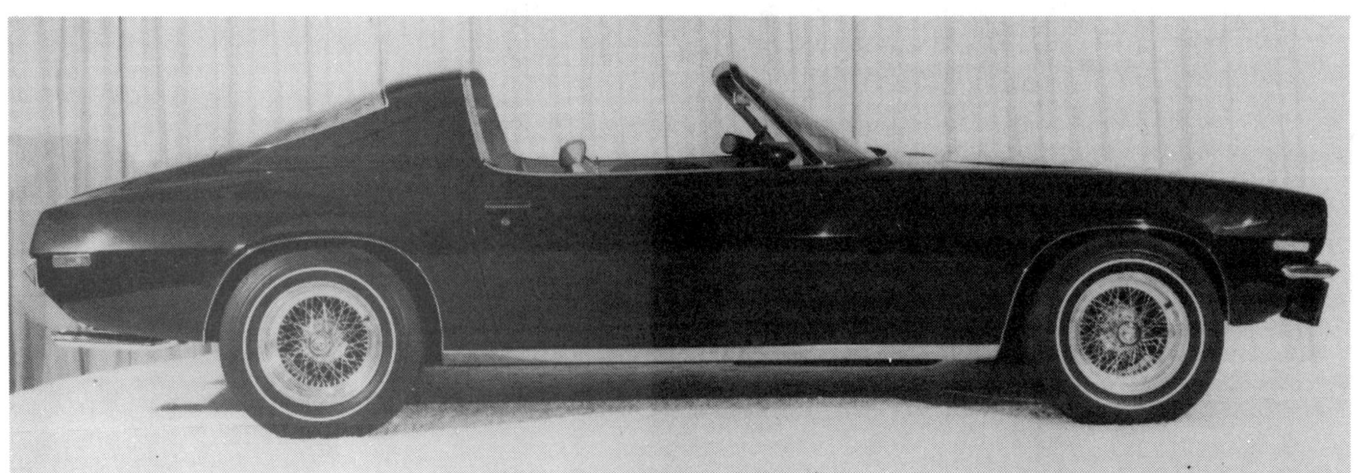

Landau show car predicted T-bar roof option which arrived much later.

Graphic magazine put it. For instance, you could no longer order the hairy, lumpy-idling 302-cid engine (Z-28s now used a 350). Four-wheel disc brakes were out. Obvious "performance" add-ons like a front air dam or an air-gulping "bubble hood" were also canned. In general, the revised Camaro was more refined, softer, and quieter than the 1967-69 models.

There were two reasons for this, as *SCG* noted: "The major one is government [which will probably] drop the guillotine on super cars and factory-installed performance equipment. Since Chevrolet doesn't like to be told what to do, they're getting the jump on our legislators . . . Reason number two is that performance equipment is expensive, and since SCCA changed its rules regarding availability of options for Trans-Am Championship racing, manufacturers aren't required to produce 'X' number of parts."

With these "givens," here's what Chevrolet engineers did do for the 1970½ Camaro. First, the steering linkage was completely redesigned, and located ahead of, rather than behind, the front ball joints. Suspension compliance was revised to better deflect road shocks and create final understeer. This made it harder to hang the tail out on the new model than on a '69. (It *was* still possible, though, if you worked at it.) The rear suspension was changed, too: multi-leaf rear springs replaced the single-leaf ones, the rear shocks were staggered to reduce rear wheel wind-up, and new spring bushings were developed to prevent lateral shake and body roll. On top of this, Z-28 and SS cars all had a special "high-effort" steering gear, which reduced the tendency to overcorrect.

The overall result was a supple, forgiving suspension. *Car and Driver* magazine went so far as to pronounce the Camaro's handling "probably the best Detroit has ever produced. The transition as you enter a curve or change is extremely predictable and this, combined with a low body roll angle, is the essence of good *road* handling." But, *C/D* went on, "In more demanding situations, those which you would encounter on a race track or perhaps on a road you had all to yourself, the Camaro is disappointing. It understeers heavily; sometimes you can trick it and get the tail out, sometimes you just have to slow down until the front tires regain their hold on the pavement." Quite a contradiction in the same paragraph. Most reviewers, however, judged the new suspension one of the best conventional layouts around.

Even more important than the chassis changes was something glossed over by most road testers, though all of them commented on the quietness of the revamped Camaro. Chevrolet had gone through an exhaustive re-engineering process to improve sound isolation in the new body to give it an extremely "tight"

Optioning Your Camaro

STANDARD TRIM
One-piece front bumper, chrome rocker moldings, steel wheels with small hubcaps, exposed wipers (matte-black finish), engine badges when equipped with 350 V-8.

STYLE TRIM GROUP (RPO Z-21)
Color-keyed door handles, double bright moldings around taillamps, bright roof gutter moldings, rear hood molding, $52.70.

RALLY SPORT (RPO Z-22)
Split front bumpers flanking grille with body-color urethane frame, parking lamps inboard of headlamps, hidden wipers, RS identification, $168.55.

SUPER SPORT (RPO Z-27)
Blacked-out grille, hidden wipers, bright engine dress-up, F70-14 white-letter tires on 7-inch wheels, chromed dual exhaust extensions, SS identification, 300-bhp 350-cid V-8 (396-cid engines optional), F-41 heavy-duty suspension, $289.65.

ADDITIONAL OPTIONS
Special Interior (Accent) Group: woodgrain instrument panel and steering wheel appliques, lower door panel carpeting, additional sound insulation, glovebox light, trunk mat, special vinyl-and-cloth upholstery, $21.10.
Special Instrument Cluster (mandatory Z-28): oil pressure and temperature gauges, ammeter, tachometer, clock, $84.30.
Console (woodgrain trim with Special Interior), $59.00.

1970 styling was good enough to stand the test of time.

Rear end bears resemblance to the '68 Corvette.

feel. For example, many of the usual welding-access holes through which components are attached during assembly were systematically eliminated. Those that were left were located away from channels and pockets where noise could get through to the interior. Also, there were fewer resonance-sensitive body panels, new sealing at panel joints, reworked side window seals, and a big layer of acoustical material sandwiched between the roof and headliner. These details made the new body one of the tightest ever produced in Detroit. The total reduction in noise from all sources was 84 percent, against, for example, just 28 percent on the 1967-69 Camaro.

Riding the same 108-inch wheelbase as before, the new Camaro was unveiled in late February 1970. Despite the fact that none of its body panels interchanged with the first generation, its dimensions were little changed—just two inches longer, a tad wider, an inch lower. Of course, the new car *was* different in many ways, and mostly for the better. For example, overall glass area had been increased 10 percent, despite the lack of quarter windows. About the worst thing you could say of the new design was that the doors were very long and bulky, but as we have already learned, there were reasons for this.

The engine lineup was narrower, and there were considerable changes in detail specs. Against 12 offerings for 1969, there were only seven for 1970½. The base six was now the 155-bhp 250-cid unit, the 230 having been banished. The base V-8 was still the 200-bhp 307, with a special 360-bhp 350 V-8 for the Z-28. One 327, two 396s, and the 427 from 1969 were missing. The factory spec sheets listed an eighth powerplant: 454 cubic inches, 450 bhp, and 500 foot-pounds of torque. But this was never actually available. And the "396" was really a 402 now, because of a minor bore increase. Chevrolet didn't list it as such: the magic number "396" had earned a following, and the sales people felt it ought to be retained.

Exterior and interior options were similar to previous Camaro offerings. Style Trim, RS, SS, and Z-28 packages were all continued, and there were two upgraded interiors, "Special" and "Custom." One interesting distinction was that standard (and even Style Trim) models had exposed wipers. To get the optional hidden wipers you had to order the Rally Sport equipment. This also gave you a freestanding grille with a urethane-covered frame and split front bumper, parking lights mounted inboard of the headlights *a la* Jaguar XJ, special badges, plus the Style Trim group. As before, the more functional SS equipment could be ordered with or without the RS appearance features (see sidebar). Hardly anyone specified the bench seat on the 1967-69 cars, so buckets were now standard.

Buyers really had to wield the option book to fill up that dashboard. The only standard instruments were a speedometer and fuel gauge. Warning lights looked after all other functions. The gauge package, mandatory for Z-28s, replaced the blanked-off holes with needle instruments for less than $100. The console, too, was optional at $59.

For the most part, the second-generation Camaro was greeted favorably. "A tremendous improvement," was how *Road & Track* magazine saw it. "Puts the Ponycar in a new class." Its big complaint was about the brakes. If anything, they were even less fade-resistant than those of earlier models. They were judged adequate for daily use and emergencies, but marginal for vigorous downhill mountain work, a fairly limited criticism. Also, in *R&T's* opinion, the Camaro was too big for its passenger and cargo capacity. "But overall it's a pleasant, responsive, solid car—very nice to drive in the day-in-day-out routine, and an exceedingly good long-distance touring car. In fact, we'll have to say it's the best American car we've ever driven, and more importantly, it's one of the most satisfying cars for all-around use we've every driven."

R&T has often tagged various cars as the best ever driven, so these musings can be taken with the cautionary grain of salt. What this evaluation suggested, though, was a very important achievement. After a decade or so of trying, America had finally produced a *gran turismo* in the true sense of the term: a road car able to carry two passengers and their luggage for long distances in great comfort—rapidly. And thanks to Bill Mitchell's unerring sense of style, it was marvelous to look at.

The Camaro Model and Engine Lineup for 1970½

Model	Base Price	Weight	Production
Six-cylinder coupe	$2749	3076	12,566
V-8 coupe	$2839	3190	112,323

Engine	cid	Bore × Stroke	bhp @ rpm	C.R. (:1)
Base Six	250	3.875 × 3.53	155 @ 4200	8.5
Base V-8	307	3.875 × 3.25	200 @ 4600	9.0
Z-28 V-8	350	4.00 × 3.48	360 @ 6000	11.0
Opt. V-8	350	4.00 × 3.48	250 @ 4800	9.0
Opt. V-8	350	4.00 × 3.48	300 @ 4800	10.25
Opt. V-8	396	4.126 × 3.76	350 @ 5200	10.25
Opt. V-8	396	4.126 × 3.76	375 @ 5600	11.0

Driving Impressions: 1972 Sport Coupe

Ray Dunn's green-gold '72 Camaro is the most luxurious of the four cars driven and photographed for our driving impressions features. And being a '72, it's also one of the rarest. Less than 70,000 were built, because of a strike at the Norwood, Ohio factory (see Chapter IV).

By and large, the '72 was a close copy of the '71, though there were some distinguishing differences. The grille on standard models had a coarser texture, with seven instead of twelve vertical slats, and was more eggcrate than mesh. Three-point shoulder belts were standard for the first time. The interior door panels were markedly changed, and now sported commodious storage compartments. There was even a coin holder under the door handle on the driver's side.

This car is fitted with automatic transmission controlled by the "stirrup" shifter on the optional console. That console is wide enough to make the front compartment feel a bit tight, but it does provide a second storage locker. No extra instruments are fitted here, and the dashboard looks a little vacant without them. A large speedometer and an equal-size (and relatively enormous) fuel gauge, and that's it. Four smaller holes, two on each side of the centrally placed main dials, are where the optional instruments would go, but here house warning lights. A vertical slot between the fuel gauge and speedo contains the shift quadrant, while lights and wiper/washer knobs, plus the cigarette lighter, are located at the outer ends of the instrument cluster. The entire dash is finished in

Subject car is equipped the way most buyers ordered their Camaros in the early '70s.

Standard '72 grille has more open look.

Second generation looks teriffic from any angle.

Handy bins were added to '72 doors.

Dash seems bare without optional gauges.

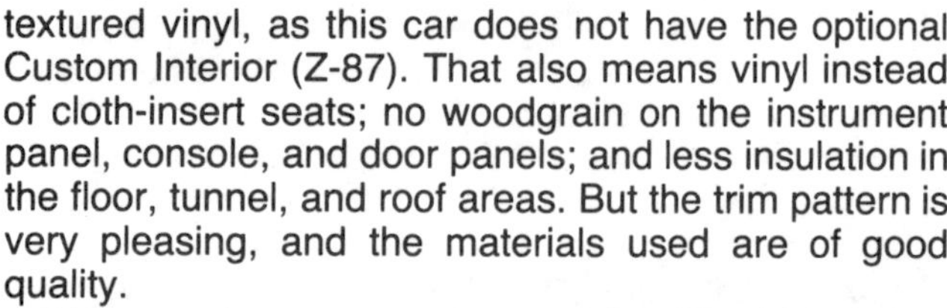

textured vinyl, as this car does not have the optional Custom Interior (Z-87). That also means vinyl instead of cloth-insert seats; no woodgrain on the instrument panel, console, and door panels; and less insulation in the floor, tunnel, and roof areas. But the trim pattern is very pleasing, and the materials used are of good quality.

This car is set up as a comfortable high-speed tourer, so naturally it has the optional air conditioning, integrated with the powerful heater/defroster. This system allows the driver to select almost any climate at a touch of the appropriate lever. Flow-through "Astro Ventilation," with air extractor vents hidden in the door jambs, is highly effective. All in all, this is a very comfortable car, as long as you're in one of the front seats. The Camaro follows ponycar tradition with a back seat that's little more than a temporary perch for adults.

Despite its relative rarity, this '72 is typical of the way most Camaros were ordered in the early '70s: 307 V-8 (the 396 wasn't available that year for California buyers like Dunn anyway), automatic transmission, standard

Optional console provided extra glove locker.

Stylish dash wasn't changed until 1979.

Standard chassis delivers a soft ride, modest body roll, and some front-end plow.

suspension, standard disc/drum brake system, and power steering. Out of 68,656 units built during the 1972 model run, nearly 64,000 were V-8s, about 60,000 had power steering, and nearly 58,000 had automatic. Air conditioning, though less common, was installed in almost half of all Camaros that year. So, it's safe to say that this sort of equipment is what the majority of Camaro buyers wanted.

What sort of *car* did they get? Basically, a "personal" car, not something you'd use for a double date. This engine and transmission combination gives good low-range acceleration, literally any cruising speed you want up to about 85 mph (above which the car gets pretty noisy), and returns from 12 to 16 miles per gallon.

The stock suspension is supple and cushy, hardly the underpinnings of a NASCAR champion. This is an understeering car, so it tends to plow a lot in hard corners. But it should be noted that it handles well, *if* you're comparing it to the typical American car of the period rather than to a Z-28 or Shelby-Mustang. Like all second-generation Camaros, it hunkers down low on

Air extractor vents live in rear of door jambs.

Long doors can be clumsy in crowded places.

Back seat is better used for luggage than people.

Base 307 V-8 has ample passing power, runs quietly.

the road, and gives a ground-hugging appearance from all angles.

Brakes are the standard 11-inch front discs and 9.5-inch rear drums, which we find perfectly adequate for all but severe driving conditions—like going flat-out down Pikes Peak, for example. We've never been too concerned about claims in various road tests that Camaro brakes weren't up to snuff. Perhaps one driver in a hundred drove hard enough to induce fade. Obviously, anybody ordering power steering, automatic, and air was not too interested in how many fractions of a "g" the car would pull in a tight corner.

Over the road, this 1972 Camaro is beautifully smooth, and has ample power for passing. But what is most impressive about it, especially with this particular drivetrain, is its uncanny silence. For a car in its price class, it must have been a revelation when new, especially compared to the somewhat noisier Mustangs and Cougars. It was no better at carrying four people than they were, but again, that wasn't its main purpose. Some reviewers were always bemoaning the lack of rear seat room in ponycars. Our wager is that if a Camaro's back seat was used 10 percent of the time (and most weren't), then it might be a problem. But considered as a two-seater, the coupe earns high marks for comfort, and has more than adequate luggage capacity if you count the back seat as additional cargo room.

We can't help thinking, though, that this really seems a very large car. Perhaps that's because there are so many more smaller cars on the roads now than in '72, making the size difference more noticeable. We found ourselves wondering what the Camaro would be like scaled down to, say, 80 percent of its exterior size. Inside, front seat room could be preserved by eliminating the back seat, rather like AMC did when creating the AMX out of the Javelin. It would be interesting. Come to think of it, the new '82 model will have similar dimensions, though it will retain a vestigial back seat.

Stylewise, there's little to fault in the '72, or indeed any second-generation Camaro. All the lines are right. One possible exception on this car is the two-tone effect of the vinyl roof. The plastic covering is still a popular add-on, and reflects contemporary tastes the way tailfins did in the '50s. On the Camaro, it doesn't look all *that* out of place (other cars fare much worse: the Lincoln Versailles, for example) but the unadorned shape is so pure that it somehow seems unfair to break up its lines with a vinyl roof.

Incidentally, Mr. Dunn's car shows over 88,000 miles on the odometer. Would you have guessed it?

SPECIFICATIONS

DIMENSIONS

Wheelbase: 108 inches. **Length:** 189 inches. **Width:** 75 inches. **Height:** 52 inches. **Weight:** 3248 pounds.

ENGINE

Type: ohv, 90-degree V-8. **Bore-and-Stroke:** 3.875×3.25 inches. **Displacement:** 307 cubic inches. **Rated bhp:** 190 gross @ 4200 rpm, 130 net @ 4000 rpm. **Net torque:** 230 foot-pounds @ 2400 rpm.

TRANSMISSION

Two-speed Powerglide automatic. **Gear ratios:** 1.82:1 (1st), 1.00:1 (2nd). **Rear axle ratio:** 3.08:1.

CHASSIS

Unitized body/chassis. **Front suspension:** independent with unequal-length A-arms, coil springs, tubular shocks. **Rear suspension:** live axle with semi-elliptic leaf springs and tubular shocks. **Brakes:** disc front, drums rear, 332 square inches total swept area. **Steering:** power-assisted recirculating ball gear (linkage located ahead of front axle centerline), 15.5:1 overall ratio, 3.5 turns lock-to-lock, 38 ft. turning circle.

PERFORMANCE

0-30 mph, seconds: 5.6
0-60 mph, seconds: 11.3
0-80 mph, seconds: 16:5
Standing-start quarter mile: 17 seconds @ 85 mph.
Speeds in gears (mph): 63 (1st), 105 (2nd).
Fuel consumption: 12-16 mpg, average 14.5

Camaro in the '70s
Persistence Pays Off

Ponycar popularity was on the wane by the time the all-new 1970 Camaro arrived, and GM began to consider whether it should continue the line beyond the normal three-year cycle (1970-72). There was, primarily, a question of whether the plant was justified. Camaros and Firebirds were built along side Novas at Norwood, Ohio (there was also a west coast factory at Van Nuys, California). Given the decrease in ponycar sales, questions were raised about Norwood's long-term viability; perhaps, some thought, it should turn out only Novas.

The situation reached a climax in April 1972, when the United Auto Workers union called a strike at Norwood, stopping production for almost six months. The union was protesting layoffs that had occurred as F-body sales continued to soften. As a result, Camaro production for the calendar year came to 63,832—a record low. After the strike, Nova production was transferred for fear that any further work stoppages at Norwood would hurt the compact's sales, which were still strong. This move only dimmed the F-body's prospects for survival.

External appearance was unchanged for 1971. High-back bucket seats were adapted from Vega.

Without Rally Sport option, SS models carried grille insignia.

What saved the Camaro and Firebird was a determined in-house "public relations" effort by Chevrolet and Pontiac executives, who thought the cars were too good to lose. Their argument to GM brass was that, even though sales weren't what they once were, these cars were of strategic importance, especially to dealers. Because they were quite different from rank-and-file Chevy and Pontiac models (except maybe for the Corvette), they got people into the showrooms. Fortunately, the lobbying campaign worked, and the Camaro/Firebird got a reprieve.

Like many GM decisions, this proved to be a good move. For one thing, the ponycar ranks were shrinking. Mustang evolved into the smaller 1974 Mustang II. Cougar became a specialty offering in the Montego line. The Barracuda/Challenger vanished after 1974. And, the Javelin got rather controversial styling which carried it to its demise after 1975. With all this, GM suddenly found that keeping the Camaro and Firebird around was not only practical, but also positively desirable. Suddenly, they were the only *true* ponycars left. At first, sales didn't pick up, mostly because of the drop in demand for performance cars caused by the 1973-74 oil crisis. But after gas started flowing again,

With Rally Sport option, SS emblem appeared on fenders only.

Styling prototype, probably for '72. Note square parking lamps inboard of headlights.

the buyers came back. By 1977, Camaro model year production was up over the 200,000 mark, a level it hadn't reached since 1969. In 1978, a record 272,631 cars were built.

For 1971-72, Camaro was very little changed. Rolling with Federal regulations, it was modified just enough to comply with emissions and crash protection laws. You could spot the '71 at a glance by looking at the seats—high-back buckets with built-in headrests taken straight out of the Vega (the '70s had their own low-back seats with separate headrests). Items that are easy and cheap to change, like hubcaps, color schemes, and upholstery, were shifted, and the Z-28 got a front air dam plus a redesigned rear deck spoiler.

Also beginning in 1971, GM switched to SAE net horsepower ratings, instead of quoting gross horsepower for its engines. This hardly made the advertising agency's job of promoting the Camaro as a performance car any easier. The 250-cid six was now listed at 110 net horsepower (against 145 gross in 1970). The 402 (née 396) came down to a lowly 240 bhp net. Many of the performance engines, such as the 350- and 375-bhp 396s, were dropped. Cloth-and-vinyl replaced all-vinyl as the standard upholstery material,

Standard-trim models got a revised grille with bigger eggcrates for '72.

and the usual assortment of RS and SS appearance and performance packages were carried over.

For 1972—when the crippling Norwood strike made it look like the Camaro's number was up—changes were again minor. Standard models got a facial alteration by the simple measure of having fewer vertical bars, producing larger "eggcrates" and a more aggressive look (the split-grille RS front end was unchanged). Three-point shoulder belts were installed at Washington's behest for the first time, and during the production run a "fasten seatbelts" warning light was added to the dashboard. Another minor change was

Second-generation shape looked best in no-frills form.

1973 Type LT with standard grille

Modest badge to right of grille identified LT.

LT replaces SS in 1973 line, reflected waning performance-car market.

new colors for the vinyl roof option, which was now finished in gloss. Engine power ratings stayed about the same.

For 1973, there were new bumper-impact regulations, but Chevy managed to hold on to the Camaro's front end styling without resorting to the "rubber baby buggy bumpers" adopted by some other car makers. This was done by moving both front and rear bumpers farther away from the body, and reinforcing them with brackets, braces, and an inner support bar.

The trend away from performance was underlined this year by the arrival of the Type LT (Luxury Touring)

Pre-production 1973 LT with Rally Sport option at proving ground press preview

Type LT cost $400 extra, but was worth the money.

Camaros would remain fine handlers throughout the '70s.

Early version of Bill Mitchell's Berlinetta. Car carried 427 aluminum-block Corvette engine.

Sloped front with "sugar scoop" lights appeared for '74.

Comfy cloth-covered interior of the '74 Type LT.

New wraparound taillights on '74 models eliminated need for rear side markers.

The elegant solution to Federal bumper regulations

Wraparound rear window marked the 1975 editions.

as a replacement for the SS. The LT delivered a 165-bhp V-8, variable-ratio power steering, and appearance touches like hidden wipers, black-painted rockers and accents, streamlined "sport" mirrors, Rally wheels, and a woodgrain dashboard. It also came with the full set of instruments, deluxe upholstery, and considerably more insulation than other Camaros. Against a base price of $2872 for the standard V-8 coupe, the LT listed at $3268, but the extra $400 was probably well spent.

Prices started to gallop in 1974, with a jump of almost $500 across the board. This year saw the first

Rally Sport was revived as an exterior appearance option for mid-1975.

1975 Rally Sport featured liberal use of matte-black paint. Most had color-matched wheels shown here.

'74 front-end styling was left alone for 1975.

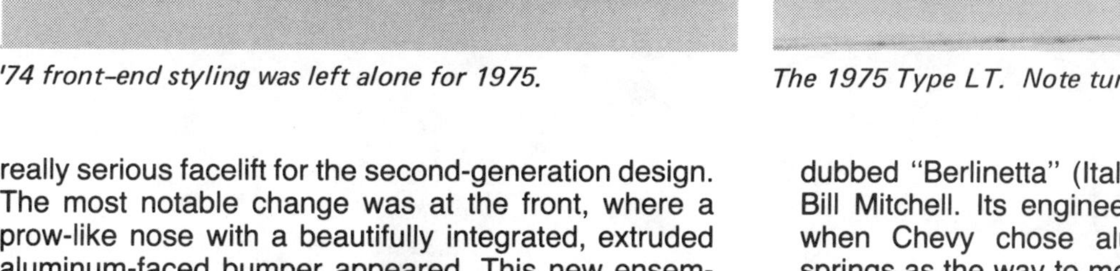

The 1975 Type LT. Note turbine-spoke wheels.

really serious facelift for the second-generation design. The most notable change was at the front, where a prow-like nose with a beautifully integrated, extruded aluminum-faced bumper appeared. This new ensemble made the car about eight inches longer than the '73. Its design roots are found in a 1970 show car dubbed "Berlinetta" (Italian for "little sedan") built for Bill Mitchell. Its engineering origins date from 1972, when Chevy chose aluminum bars over flat leaf springs as the way to meet the '74 bumper standards. The rear end of the '74 was also altered to accommodate new deeper bumpers and a revised back panel with smooth, wraparound taillights that eliminated the need for the rear side marker beacons.

Overall, this was extremely deft handling of Federal mandates. It eliminated what Bill Mitchell called the "ugly, dirty black bumpers . . . the asphalt stage—dirty tennis shoes." And with a car like the Camaro around, automakers could no longer blame Washington for clumsy "safety car" styling. It was the beginning of a design renaissance that continues today. Detroit had stopped fighting the regulations, and was learning to live with them.

The LT became more luxurious and more costly for

You'd be hard pressed to distinguish a '75 (left) from a '76 (right) by the front end alone.

LT gained a brushed-aluminum rear applique for '76.

Few changes occurred for 1977. All models now had hidden wipers. This is the Type LT.

'74 (now over $3700 base), and the 307 V-8 was dropped from the engine chart in favor of a detoxed 350 with 145 net horsepower, except in California. This was one year when Californians came out better than buyers in the other 49 states: their base version of the 350 had a four-barrel carburetor, good for 155 bhp.

The most significant appearance alteration on the 1975 Camaro was a new wraparound rear window nicely blended into the original greenhouse lines. In fact, the idea had been developed even before the second-generation design was introduced. Sales picked up to the 150,000-unit level again, giving

The 1974 facelift continued through '77. Changes throughout were again minor.

Camaro Engines (displacement/net horsepower) 1971-80

	1971	1972	1973	1974	1975	1976	1977	1978	1979	1980
Base Six, cid	250	250	250	250	250	250	250	250	250	229
bhp	110	110	100	100	105	105	110[1]	110[1]	115[1]	115[5]
Base V-8, cid	307	307	307	350	350	305	305	305	305	267
bhp	140	130	115	145[2]	145[2]	140	145	145	130	120
Z-28/V-8, cid	350	350	350	350			350	350	350	350[6]
bhp	275	255	245	245			185[3]	185[3]	175[4]	190
Opt. V-8, cid	350	350	350	350	350	350	350	350	350	305
bhp	165	165	145	185	155	165	170	170	170	155
Opt. V-8, cid	350	350	350							
bhp	210	200	175							
Opt. V-8, cid	402	402								
bhp	260	240								
Cal. V-8, cid				350	350		305	305	305	
bhp				160	155		135	135	125	
Cal. V-8, cid							350	350	350	
bhp							160	160	165	

1 = 90-bhp in California; 2 = n.a. California; 3 = 175-bhp Cal. or hi-altitude; 4 = 170-bhp Cal. or hi-altitude; 5 = 110-bhp 231-cid V-6 Cal.; 6 = 165-bhp, 305-cid V-8 Cal.

Chevy's ponycar a firm lease on life. Despite its styling refinements, this was now a five-year-old design—yet it had been so good in the first place that it looked entirely up to date.

Capitalizing on the Camaro's renewed popularity, Chevy revived the Rally Sport package as a mid-season exterior appearance option (RPO Z-85) priced at $238. It was very splashy: matte-black paint covered the hood and front fender tops, swept back past the cowl just below the side windows, and then up to cover most of the roof. For the rest of the body you had a choice of white, metallic blue, silver, red, or bright canary yellow. When wearing color-matched Z-28 Trans-Am wheels, the new RS was certainly unmistakable.

Other new-for-'75 features were the first catalytic converter, finned rear brake drums, twin-exhaust mufflers on V-8s, High-Energy Ignition for all models, a passel of new audio equipment, optional power door locks and cruise control, and the availability of air conditioning on six-cylinder models for the first time.

For 1976-77, the '74 facelift just kept going, as Camaro reached, then exceeded, its old sales record of the '60s. Most styling changes for '76 centered on the popular Type LT. This gained a textured vinyl (instead of woodgrain) instrument panel and a

The 1978 Sport Coupe shows off the year's new shovel-nose front with body-color bumpers.

Tri-color taillamps debuted on '78s. License plate was placed below new body-color bumper.

brushed-aluminum rear panel appliqué. For 1977, the LT offered bright new woven-cloth upholstery instead of the plaid material previously used (vinyl continued as an alternative). Hidden wipers became standard for all models. But the big item was the somewhat surprising return of the Z-28 for 1977½.

This new Z-28, which continued through the 1981 model year, was designed around a much different set of priorities. Instead of producing a fire-breathing speed machine (which would have been hard to certify in an age of desmogged engines and fuel economy standards), Chevy created a true road car with the emphasis on handling. (Details are found in our driving impressions of the 1978 Z-28.)

Another substantial styling shakeup occurred for '78, and the Camaro came out looking even more like Mitchell's Berlinetta show car. The reworked nose carried grillework above and below a faired-in, body-color bumper. Out back were wider, tri-color taillamps set against a black or silver rear-end panel. There were new interiors and new colors inside and out. A milestone was marked as Camaro number 2-million was produced on May 11, 1978. Although a wide range of options was offered, the engine lineup was not nearly as broad as it had once been, and prices were a lot higher:

Berlinetta replaced LT as the top-of-the-line Camaro for 1979.

The splashy Rally Sport put in its last appearance in 1980.

Berlinetta got a finer grille mesh, standard V-6 power for 1980.

	Six	V-8
Sport coupe	$4414	$4599
Rally Sport	4784	4965
LT	4814	4999
LT Rally Sport	5065	5250
Z-28	—	5604

The Style Trim package continued as a $70 option for all models.

LT became "Berlinetta" for 1979, as GM finally adopted the name which had graced various Ferraris, that Camaro show car, and a European Opel Manta model. (GM photographs reveal the name was considered for an option package proposed for the late-'69/early-'70 first-generation cars.) The main styling change occurred inside: the concave-oval instrument panel was finally revised—the old dies had simply worn out! Its replacement retained the same basic layout and instrument location, but had a wider, squarer upper portion which incorporated ventilation outlets plus lights and wiper/washer switches. The heater controls and radio were still mounted below the main cluster.

For 1980, the same basic confection was back again. Camaro was now pretty thirsty compared to most other GM cars, but was as popular as ever. Four versions were cataloged: standard coupe, RS, Berlinetta, and Z-28, with base prices ranging from $5499 to $7121. Standard this year was a smaller, Chevy-built 229-cid V-6 with 110 bhp, replacing the less thrifty 250-incline six. This new engine, available in all models save the Z-28, gave its best performance when mated to the four-speed manual transmission, although it was no powerhouse to begin with. For *real* performance, there was still no choice but the Z-28. And despite everything that had been legislated to discourage such cars, this Camaro would still turn 0-60 mph times of less than 10 seconds—quite something for a Federally approved 1980 car.

CAMARO MODEL YEAR PRODUCTION, 1971-80

Year	Z-28	Other V-8	Six	Total
1971	4,862	98,590	11,191	114,643
1972	2,575	61,257	4,824	68,656
1973	11,574	81,564	3,618	96,756
1974	13,802	115,008	22,198	151,008
1975	—	116,430	29,359	145,789
1976	—	144,934	38,047	182,981
1977	14,349	173,115	31,390	218,854
1978	54,907	180,742	36,982	272,631
1979	84,879	175,779	21,913	282,571
1980	45,143	55,758	51,104	152,005

Camaro

Color Gallery II

Rolling off the assembly line, 1974

1972 SS

1972 SS

1974 Type LT

1975 Type LT

1977 Z-28

1977 Type LT

1978 Z-28

1978 Sport Coupe

1978 Z-28 (Owner: Stephen J. Wheeler)

1978 Z-28 (Owner: Stephen J. Wheeler)

1979 Berlinetta

1980 Z-28

1981 Z-28

1981 Berlinetta

Driving Impressions: 1978 Z-28

Latter-day Z-28s (the 1977-81 models) are a very different breed than their early-'70s predecessors. So, it's best to begin this report with a rundown of how the high-performance Camaro evolved during the decade. The second-generation cars may be divided into two groups: 1970-74, and 1977-81. (The Z-28 was in limbo for 1975-76.)

The 1970 edition received a new powerplant, a smooth 360-horsepower version of the 350 V-8, derived from the Corvette LT-1 unit. This engine used a forged-steel crankshaft and four-bolt main bearings. The carburetor was a Holley four-barrel, fitted to an aluminum high-rise manifold. Mechanical valve lifters, heads from the 302, chrome dress-up kit, and high-capacity radiator were all standard. The chassis was essentially unchanged from 1969, though a thicker front anti-roll bar was used. Some '70s can be distinguished by their low-profile rear spoilers, similar to the 1967-69 design, which was phased out after 1971 in favor of the taller integrated version that continued through 1981.

In performance, the '70 was every bit as hot as its

Revived Z stayed mostly the same for '78, except for grille.

Low-back bucket seats identify this as a 1970 Z-28.

1971 Z-28 was exempt from GM's low-compression-ratio edict.

predecessors—some said even hotter. But it was not the lumpy-idling machine the '69 was—not by a long shot. The new Z-28 was marked by turbine-like smoothness, mainly because the 350 was not a thinly disguised racing engine, as was the 302. Rather, it was designed with an eye to the government's emission limits, which would become more and more exacting over the next several years.

The government's widening influence on car design was seen in the Z-28 for 1971. That year the industry responded to critics of the "horsepower race" by advertising engine output in SAE net (rather than gross) figures. GM also adopted a self-imposed limit on compression ratios (not higher than 8.5:1) so its cars would run on leaded or low-lead regular gas. The Z-28, Pontiac Trans Am, and Corvette were exempt, however, and used 9:1 compression. Even so, the horsepower of the Camaro's 350 V-8 came down to 330 gross, or 275 net.

Through 1974, horsepower ratings kept sliding as emission controls began strangling performance engines. Net power fell to 255 bhp for 1972, and slipped to 245 for 1973-74. Very few engine modifications were made during this time, except for the addition of hydraulic lifters in 1972. The steering ratio, which had varied often through the years, stayed at 16:1, with power assist mandatory.

By de-emphasizing the performance aspects of the Z-28, Chevy was eventually able to reduce the cost of the package. The option sold for nearly $800 in 1971; by 1973 it was down to $500. Contributing to the cut was the decision to drop the expensive high-rise

Chevy switched to hydraulic lifters for '72 Z.

Most 1970–74 Zs had wide hood and decklid stripes.

Front air dam became standard on '72 Z-28s. This one also has RS option.

aluminum manifold after 1972. Another sign that things weren't quite what they used to be was the disappearance of the "drag-strip" 4.10:1 rear axle ratio in 1973. Also that year, Positraction became a standard item, and the first Z-cars with air conditioning were produced.

Very little changed for the 1974 edition, although "High-Energy" solid-state ignition came along at mid-year. Mechanical differences were limited to making power steering a standard Z item, and use of aluminum cases for all four-speed transmissions. The '74s were decorated with bright new hood and rear deck graphics, and had black-painted grillework outlined in silver.

In 1974, one GM executive summarized, the company decided to "kill the car before it died a slow, lingering death." The Arab oil embargo, which created block-long waiting lines at every gas-short service station, suddenly made the Z-28 almost unsaleable. Even after Camaro sales as a whole began recovering toward the end of the model year, GM was reluctant to continue the Z-car. It would have to overcome the strictest emissions limits yet, plus meet new noise standards. The expense of bringing the car into compliance seemed just too great in view of its questionable sales potential. Thus, the Z-28 was abruptly and unceremoniously dropped.

Why, then, was it brought back in mid-1977? Mainly it was a marketing decision, though thousands of enthusiasts applauded the move. During 1974 and 1975, the Camaro had returned to the competition lists, running with distinction in the International Race of

After a two-year hiatus, Z-28 returned in mid-1977 as a road car.

Champions (IROC) in the hands of its old friends at Penske Racing. With this kind of a publicity spin-off, it made sense to return the Z-28 to the showrooms. Cleverly, however, GM did not pick up where it had left off and build a street version of a racer. Instead, the production Z was revived as a grand tourer, able to hold its own with the best of Europe. Though the focus was now clearly on handling, Chevy engineers gave it as much get-up-and-go as they possibly could, given the state of emissions technology in the late '70s.

IROC competition (1978 event shown) helped bring back the Z.

Here's what turned a '77 Camaro into the reborn Z.

A quartet of IROC Camaros in 1978.

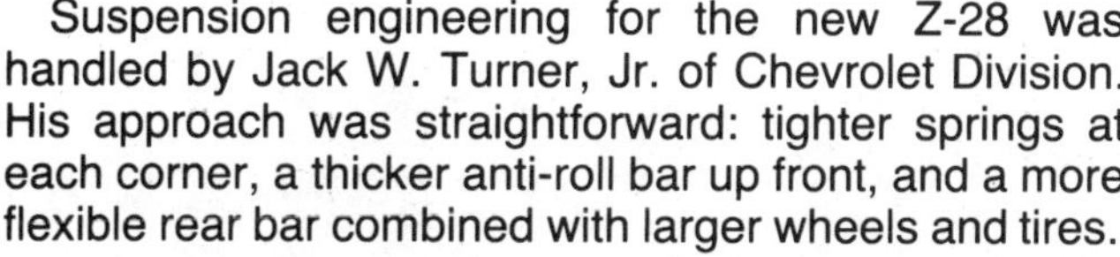

Suspension engineering for the new Z-28 was handled by Jack W. Turner, Jr. of Chevrolet Division. His approach was straightforward: tighter springs at each corner, a thicker anti-roll bar up front, and a more flexible rear bar combined with larger wheels and tires.

"We had a number of ways to go," Turner put it.*

---

* *From an interview with Michael Lamm,* op cit. *Used by permission.*

Slopeback nose, wraparound taillights marked '78 facelift.

New '78 back panel carried tri-color taillamps.

'78 nose treatment makes front end look great.

Z-28's Trans Am wheels are keyed to body color.

From this angle, a car that's wild yet graceful.

Still potent 350 V-8 delivers '60s-style go.

Big, wide doors ease entry to low-set pilot's seat.

"We could put roll stiffness into the vehicle with just stabilizer bars, but then it's not too good on tramp input . . . We tried to pick a happy medium between going up in spring rates and still not having to add humongous stabilizer bars. We tried to balance the system so the car could go over road undulations and go into corners with chatter bumps so that the suspension would allow the tires to envelope some of that roughness . . . That means a lot of refinement between the shock valving, spring rate, and stabilizer bar rate."

Turner also gave the car faster steering, with a 13.02:1 ratio compared to 14.3:1 on the '74. The wheels were 15 × 7 inches, the tires Goodyear GR70-15 steel-belted radials. The engine was the relatively tame, 185-bhp (net) version of the 350 breathing through a four-barrel Rochester carburetor. The four-bolt mains, forged crank, and long-duration cam of past Z-cars were nowhere to be found.

The 1978-81 Z-28 was basically just an evolution of the 1977½ package. The '78 was almost unchanged. The '79 edition had fewer horses and new graphics, along with the new instrument panel shared with other Camaros that year. That brings us to the 1978 model you see here, spotlessly maintained by Stephen J. Wheeler.

The big doors yawned open and we sank into the driver's large, comfortable bucket seat. Glancing back, we noted that the rear seat seemed deeper and more "buckety" than we'd remembered—not as much of a bench as most tests described it. (For 1979, the back seat actually was separated by eliminating the thinly padded connecting portion over the driveshaft tunnel.) The instrument panel is the same angled oval that marked all Camaros from 1970 to '78. The smallish steering wheel has simulated string wrapping on the rim, which gives a good grip. We think four spokes are two too many, as they obscure your view of the instruments. The '78 Z-car, by the way, had the full complement of gauges as standard. They're all very legible, but we'd have been happier if the speedo and tach were a little larger to allow more space between their markings for better legibility.

The transmission here is the Borg-Warner T-10 four-speed manual, though Turbo Hydra-Matic was available and, we're told, more popular. We think we know why. There's nothing wrong with the four-speed version, except that there's hardly any place east of the Mississippi where you can properly wring it out. There's so much torque available, you can easily drive off in first and shift directly to fourth once the car gets rolling. Using the intermediate gears and a heavy foot results in speeds that are simply unacceptable to the National Highway Traffic Safety Administration, Ralph Nader, and our mothers.

In spite of all we've heard about late-model Zs being primarily "driver's cars," this '78 had more than enough straight-line performance for us. Going from rest to 60 mph takes just 7.5 seconds—real '60s hot-rod stuff, and hardly what you'd expect in a car from the late '70s. Of course, you can't do this too often unless you own an oil well. Leadfoot driving returns single-digit mpg figures, which won't exactly endear this car to conservationists.

But give the Z-28 its head on some fast turns and you get proof positive of how well the suspension engineers did their work: it sticks like glue. A slight plowing tendency only becomes apparent in extremely tight corners. On a bend at 50 mph or better, the beast just digs in and keeps gaining momentum. On one sweeping right hander, we hit the apex at about 60, jabbed the accelerator, and were doing an indicated 90 before we were out of the turn. And that was in *fourth* gear. We didn't have the nerve to try it in third, let alone second, though either of those is available at mid-range speeds. Tracking and stability on turnpike or

Front fender "gills," resited license plate were new for '78.

Fender "spats," new striping appeared on '79 edition.

Bulkier hood scoop is main clue to the 1980 Z.

The 1980 Z-28: swift, stylish survivor of the high-performance age.

superhighway were practically faultless.

Practical considerations like rear seat legroom, visibility, and trunk space seem almost secondary in a car like this, but they ought to be mentioned just for the record. There was never much room in the back of *any* Camaro, and the '78 is no exception. The somewhat broad rear roof pillars are stylish, but make life difficult when you're trying to angle into a tight parking space. The trunk is, as one of our friends put it, little more than a Lilliputian foot locker, so plan to carry most of your travel needs in the back seat. And considering today's gas prices, the appalling mileage can literally drive you to the poorhouse—if it's not too far away, that is.

In regular CONSUMER GUIDE® magazine test reports, the late-model Z-28s were rated pretty low. But because this is a publication for enthusiasts, not ordinary car buyers, we're inclined to be somewhat less critical. What the Z-car fan wants most are style and performance—and the car delivers these in abundance. This particular Z is striking in its bright yellow paint, which accents the bold graphics and aggressive details—Rally wheels, prominent spoiler, black-out grille. As a comfortable, high-speed, two-passenger GT, the Z-28 ranks among the very best this country has produced.

And yet, this is a car of sensations from a bygone world. Nestled in the dark confines of the Z's cockpit, you stare at a ridiculously calibrated (130-mph) speedometer. Grab the big, clunky shift lever and floor the throttle: instantly, you find yourself pinned to the big bucket seat by the accelerative G-forces as the car squats down and rockets away to become a tiny dot on the horizon. Such are the joys of yesteryear, when every kid wanted a car like this, and could buy one for $3000 or so. All of which makes the Z-28 something of an anachronism in today's world.

After 1981, Camaros like this will leave Chevy showrooms for good. The 1967-81 Zs will then take on the status of retired champions, driven mainly by a relative handful of enthusiasts—and not too often as gas rises toward two dollars a gallon. The sad thing is that this last survivor of the ponycar era will be gone. Only the memories will linger on. But what glorious memories they are.

SPECIFICATIONS

DIMENSIONS

Wheelbase: 108 inches. **Length:** 197.6 inches. **Width:** 74.5 inches. **Height:** 49.2 inches. **Weight:** 3590 pounds.

ENGINE

Type: ohv, 90-degree V-8. **Bore-and-Stroke:** 4.00 × 3.48 inches. **Displacement:** 350 cubic inches. **Net bhp:** 185 @ 4000 rpm. **Net torque:** 280 foot-pounds @ 2400 rpm.

TRANSMISSION

Four-speed all synchromesh gearbox. **Gear ratios:** 2.64:1 (1st), 1.75:1 (2nd), 1.34:1 (3rd), 1.00:1 (4th). **Rear axle ratio:** 3.42:1.

CHASSIS

Unitized body-chassis. **Front suspension:** independent with unequal-length A-arms, coil springs, tubular shocks, and anti-roll bar. **Rear suspension:** live axle with semi-elliptic leaf springs, tubular shocks, and anti-roll bar. **Brakes:** disc front, drums rear, 326 square inches total swept area. **Steering:** integral-assist recirculating ball gear, 2.6 turns lock-to-lock, 36.0 ft. turning circle.

PERFORMANCE

0-30 mph, seconds: 2.8
0-60 mph, seconds: 7.5
0-80 mph, seconds: 12.7
Standing-start quarter mile: 15.9 seconds @ 91 mph.
Fuel consumption: 13-16 mpg, average 14.5

Camaro Today:
1981's Fitting Finale

At this writing, the second-generation Camaro is in its 11th and final year. Quoting the attractive 1981 sales brochure (with its Art Deco cover, and sure to be a collector's item) the latest model is "sleek and crisp [with] show-stopping good looks, unmistakable zest for hugging the road and capturing the heart, and a flair for moving through life with style." Life for those 1981s that are carefully preserved will be long. As the last of a distinguished breed, they are destined to be among the prime collector's cars of the '80s.

It's been a good, long run for the smooth and sleek second generation. The '81 model looks so good it's hard to believe the basic design was on the drawing boards way back in 1968. And Chevrolet has done its best to make this valedictory edition one of the nicest. There are three versions—the basic, but very well

The 1981 Z-28. Not many cars styled in the '60s still look this good.

T–bar roof, shown on the '81 Z, became a Camaro option with the 1979 models.

equipped Sport Coupe, the luxurious Berlinetta, and the head-turning Z-28. Dropped from the '81 lineup was the Rally Sport — only a "cosmetic-performance" car in recent years.

Base power for the Sport Coupe and Berlinetta comes from Chevy's 229-cid V-6. Its 110 bhp isn't much to move around a 3400-pound car very quickly, but the V-6 will return reasonable gas mileage, especially when mated with the $133 four-speed manual gearbox. This is a much more flexible transmission than the standard three-speed manual, and well worth the investment.

The plush '81 Berlinetta with standard wire wheel covers and optional anti-theft locks.

1981 Major Options

APPEARANCE, COMFORT and CONVENIENCE

Custom Interior (standard Berlinetta): special cloth or vinyl upholstery, soft door trim with built-in armrests, integral door handles, carpeted lower door panels, $304.
Style Trim Group (standard Berlinetta): bright roof drip, lock-pillar, upper fender, hood panel and belt moldings; color-keyed door handle inserts; bright accented parking lights, $72.
Interior Decor/Quiet Sound Group (standard Berlinetta): additional instrument lighting, glovebox light, special engine compartment/hood/interior insulation, $63.
Auxiliary Lighting: ashtray, courtesy, glovebox lights (standard Berlinetta); luggage compartment and underhood lights; headlight reminder buzzer, $37.
Special Instrumentation (standard Berlinetta and Z-28): tachometer, voltmeter, water temperature gauge, electric clock, $111.

DRIVETRAIN

305-cid V-8, 4bbl (exc. Z-28): $75
267-cid V-8, 2bbl (exc. Z-28): $75
350-cid V-8, 4bbl (Z-28 automatic): NC
Four-speed manual transmission (std. Z-28): $133
Automatic Transmission: $332 (Z-28: $56)
Performance Rear Axle Ratio: $18
Positraction Limited-Slip Differential: $63
F-41 Sport Suspension: $41

INDIVIDUAL OPTIONS

Air conditioning ($525), automatic speed control (requires automatic transmission) ($123), color-keyed floor mats ($25), heavy-duty battery ($19), clock ($23), heavy-duty cooling ($33-58), rear-window defogger ($99), power door locks ($86), tinted glass ($70), halogen headlamps ($34), dual horns ($9), Sport mirrors ($43), bodyside moldings ($44), radio and radio/tape player ($90-487), rear speaker ($19), power antenna ($47), T-roof with removable glass panels ($644), adjustable driver seatback ($23), sport-cloth seats ($26), rear spoiler for Sport Coupe and Berlinetta ($57), Comfortilt steering wheel ($72), wheel cover locks for Berlinetta ($32), power windows ($133), intermittent wipers ($38).

BASE PRICES

Sport Coupe: $6780
Berlinetta: $7576
Z-28: $8263

The Sport Coupe is fitted with deep, padded vinyl bucket seats, and comes with a lot of useful standard features. There's a new, more compact Delco Freedom II battery with side terminals that is still maintenance-free. The standard power brakes have new low-drag calipers on the front discs, plus a low-weight booster, both to help improve fuel efficiency. The front discs also have audible wear sensors, which "sing" when the pads wear down and replacement is necessary. High-Energy ignition and spring rates computer selected to match each car's individual weight and equipment are carried over from 1980. Anti-corrosion measures include pre-coated steel for reinforcements, and underbody cross bars, plus the ventilated rocker panels that have been a Camaro feature from the very beginning. All Sport Coupes come with steel-belted radial tires, twin exterior "sport" mirrors (with remote control for the left one), a foam-backed vinyl headliner, center console, four-spoke steering wheel, color-keyed cut-pile carpeting, concealed windshield wipers, power steering, and a big 21-gallon fuel tank.

Priced about $800 above the Sport Coupe is the swanky Berlinetta. Here Chevrolet has gone all-out in quest of quiet by making its Quiet Sound Group standard. This includes an inner sound-absorbing roof layer, plus bottom door seals, and an inside roof covering made of soft, foam-backed material. Also standard is the Custom Trim Group, with carpeted lower doors and soft, contoured bucket seats; special courtesy lighting; and complete instrumentation from voltmeter to tachometer. Topping it all are a special striping and paint treatment, whitewalls, and wire wheel covers. There's a wheel cover locking package available, too, for theft protection, as they are *very* attractive wheels.

Of course, the Z-28 is still offered with the big 350 cubic-inch V-8 coupled to mandatory Turbo Hydra-Matic transmission. Once again, the 350 is available to California customers after a one-year absence. Also for '81, four-speed manual transmission returns, mated to the 305-cid V-8 with four-barrel carburetor (standard on Z-28, optional on other models). GM's sophisticated

This Z-28 wears still-popular Trans Am wheels.

Manual shift is again offered for '81 Z-28.

The last of a distinguished line, the 1981 Z-28 is a sure-fire collector's car of the future.

new Computer Command Control (CCC) electronic emissions-control system is found on all Camaro engines. Besides cleaning up the exhaust, it also governs engagement of the lockup torque converter on automatic-transmission models. On the Z-28, the lockup is effective on both second and third gears.

While the 305 and 350 V-8s are available in California, the optional 267 isn't. In the case of the V-6, California buyers get the Buick-built 231-cid unit instead of Chevy's 229. Both deliver 110 net horsepower, and there is little difference between them in performance or fuel mileage.

Considering that the Z-car will still deliver '60s-style acceleration and top speed, its $8300 base price (at this writing) is acceptable in today's inflation-ridden market. If you can afford the gas, it delivers the kind of driving thrill found on no other American car (except, of course, its sibling, the Pontiac Firebird Trans Am, and the Corvette). It's a wild-looking car, with a deep front air dam, graceful rear spoiler, colorful graphics, wheel opening flares and front fender louvers, hood scoop with decal, raised-white-letter tires, and body-color sport wheels.

Styling differences, other than the Z-car's flashy graphics, are very slight compared to the 1980 Camaro. Interior trim has been revised, of course, a rally steering wheel is now optional, and the speedometer has been relettered. An inexpensive but significant new option is quartz-halogen headlamps, which should really be standard on the faster models as they do wonders to improve nighttime visibility.

In this depressing year of continuing slow sales, steadily rising gasoline prices, and further challenges by sporty imports, GM could have decided not to produce the Camaro at all, let alone the Z-28. But continuity has won out, and the line will carry on with the all-new third-generation '82. Nevertheless, the '81 is a fitting finale for the second generation. Years from now, car enthusiasts not yet born when the last of these rolls off the production line will go barreling down some highway in an '81—its long hood outstretched, short deck hiding the collapsible spare tire and maybe a toothbrush, the throaty rumble from the exhaust recalling the spirit, if not the essence, of the ponycar age. For the '81, like its predecessors, is already what few cars are in their own time—a legend.

1981 Camaro Power Teams

Engine	cid	Bore × Stroke	CR	bhp @ rpm	Availability*
V-6, 2bbl	229	3.74 × 3.48	8.6	110 @ 2400	Std.-S, B
V-6, 2bbl	231	3.80 × 3.40	8.0	110 @ 3800	Std-S, B (Cal. only)
V-8, 2bbl	267	3.50 × 3.48	8.3	115 @ 4000	Opt-S, B (NA Cal.)
V-8, 4bbl	305	3.74 × 3.48	8.6	165 @ 4000	Std-Z, Opt-S, B
V-8, 4bbl	350	4.00 × 3.48	8.2	175 @ 4000	Opt-Z

* S = Sport Coupe, B = Berlinetta, Z = Z-28

Camaro Tomorrow: New Beginnings in '82

For the first time in 12 years, the Camaro will appear in all-new clothing for 1982. The third-generation design is already locked up at this writing. Running prototypes have been seen at GM's Milford, Michigan proving grounds since early 1980—through the lenses of various "unauthorized" motoring press photographers.

When the '82 program got underway there was no question the new Camaro would have to be much smaller and lighter than the second generation. (That car seemed rather small back in 1970, but rapidly changing conditions had made it look quite large by the end of the decade.) Sheetmetal and mechanical components have been completely redesigned. Overall length has been cut by 18 inches, wheelbase has shrunk to 101 inches (versus the second generation's 108), and poundage has been pared down to about 2500, compared to 3400-3500 pounds for the 1970-81

Deep air dam, smooth nose help aerodynamics and mileage. Quad lights are new.

cars. Like the front-drive J-body subcompacts, the new Camaro and its Firebird cousin are part of General Motors' $40 billion master plan that will completely revise the firm's entire product line by 1985. The F-body will still retain that designation in the corporation's now-familiar alphabet soup, but the '82 is about as similar to the '81 as a Corvette is to a Monte Carlo.

From what we've seen (which isn't much as GM's design director Chuck Jordan was not inclined to aid our speculation) the new model will preserve the essential Camaro character. In other words, it will remain a sporting car that's "right" for its time. The first generation was basically a platform—a do-it-all package with buckets and floor shift, offered with enough options so it could be almost anything the buyer wanted. The second generation reflected changing tastes: smoother, quieter, more luxurious, and more stylish. The third generation will be right in step with the new driving demands of the '80s: it will have fine performance, impeccable road manners, efficient styling, and excellent fuel mileage. It would be foolish to say the '82 will be a better car than the '81. They are two very different automobiles.

Let's describe the 1982 Camaro by first listing what has *not* changed. It's still as low as before—about 50 inches by our measurements. It's also about as wide—73 inches, give or take an inch. It retains the traditional front-engine/rear-drive layout, and remains basically a two-passenger car. The rear seating, if anything, is even more "occasional" than on the 1970-81 series. However, the rear seatback now flops down to form a cargo deck for added versatility. And, of course, the '82 will be more expensive (the inflationary spiral hasn't changed, either). Estimates now range from a base of $7000 to about $9500 for the Z-28.

And now for what's completely different. The cuts in length, wheelbase, and weight mentioned earlier mean the new Camaro will be able to get along happily with a four-cylinder engine. This standard powerplant is bound to be Pontiac's long-running 2.5-liter (151-cid) inline unit, known affectionately as the "Iron Duke," seen in the X-body compacts. In the F-body, it should deliver fuel mileage in the low 30s, while providing nearly the same performance as the old inline six, but with 100 fewer cubic inches.

Other engines will be carried over from '81, since most of the development money has been put into the new body and chassis. There will again be 4.4-liter (267-cid) and 5.0-liter (305-cid) V-8s and the 3.8-liter (229-cid) V-6 as options. The 5.7-liter (350-cid) V-8 is nearing the end of its practical life, and will undoubtedly be dropped. There may be a turbocharged, fuel-injected version of the 305 for the Z-28 (though the turbo may be reserved for Pontiac's Firebird only). Fuel injection (likely to be of the throttle-body type) will provide more precise fuel metering than a carburetor under all conditions, resulting in excellent overall mileage. With the turbocharger, the 305's horsepower

Our sneak photo of the '82 prototype shows new lift-up rear hatch.

should be about 200 bhp net—say 270-280 by the forbidden gross-horsepower rating method. Add a four-speed manual gearbox, and it's easy to see why the 1982 Z-28 could be the most exciting yet.

The 1982 model line will continue with 1981's three offerings: Sport Coupe, Berlinetta, and Z-28. As in the past, there will be a standard-trim level, a variety of upgraded interior appointments and exterior appearance features (many standard on the luxury Berlinetta), and special graphics for the Z-28. The latter may be offered with Recaro seats, which have been seen in at least one prototype. Certainly, these very fine buckets will be on the options list. Instrumentation will naturally be comprehensive on the Berlinetta and Z-28, while the base model will have fewer dials and more warning lights in the same basic dashboard.

But the best news is what we can expect in the way of suspension. Details are not fully known at this writing, but the most optimistic reports suggest completely new underpinnings front and rear. The front end (according to an October, 1980 *Automotive News* story) will have the MacPherson-strut layout as used on the X- and J-cars. Several sources predict the rear end will have trailing links located by a Panhard rod, as well as a torque tube to deal with axle wind-up. Handling packages (being developed during the winter of 1980-81) will again be offered at modest prices, and should be essential for serious drivers. Steel-belted radial tires will be standard. The Z-28 will probably have wider rubber on larger-diameter wheels, possibly 15-inch cast-aluminum jobs instead of steel 14-inchers. This should give the Z-car a definite handling edge, not to mention enhancing its looks. Four-wheel disc brakes will be an option—possibly standard on the Z-28.

The steering system has been completely redesigned, though again, details are sketchy. No doubt the rack-and-pinion mechanism from the X- and J-cars will be adopted. At the very least, there will be much better steering sensitivity, perhaps rivalling that of the best European road cars.

If you worry about all this scavenging off the corporate parts shelves, don't. It makes good economic sense for the Camaro to share components with mass-production family models, as it helps keep prices reasonable. (Remember the first-generation design?) Besides, the X-cars have capable handling and performance, plus better-than-average economy. Designing the new F-body around selected X-car pieces is an obvious way to hold down manufacturing costs.

Besides all the changes under the skin, the skin itself will be quite different. Although there's a definite flavor of the second generation in the long hood, wide doors, broad C-pillar, and roof curvature, there are a number of new details. The 1982 Camaro will switch to semi-fastback styling, with a larger backlight that leads smoothly into a short tail. The backlight and surrounding sheetmetal form a large hatch, which (along with

Third generation retains roof styling and long hood of 1970–81 Camaro.

the fold-down rear seatback) makes the car eminently more practical than before for long-distance travel. And if appearances are anything to go by, all-around visibility has been greatly improved.

The nose on the prototype shown here is probably close to what you'll see. The car is certain to have a wedge profile, reflecting what Chevy has learned with computer-assisted wind tunnel testing. Engineers say the drag coefficient will be down around 0.32, putting it ahead of the slippery Plymouth TC3/Dodge 024 coupes, and making it one of the most aerodynamic cars in America. The nose configuration is a critical factor for ensuring that Camaro's gas mileage meets 1982 CAFE (corporate average fuel economy) targets. The deep integrated air dam is thus likely to be part of the final design.

Pontiac's version of the new F-body will have hidden headlamps, while the slightly downmarket Camaro will get exposed dual rectangular units—a first for the marque. Both cars will use flexible, body-color bumpers front and rear to handle crash-protection requirements. Taillamps are blended into the back panel under the hatch opening to enhance the impression of width.

What about design elements considered and rejected for the third generation? For one thing, front-wheel drive was ruled out as unnecessary for this type of car, despite the many components shared with the X- and J-cars. By 1984 or so, the Camaro, Corvette, and Firebird will probably be the only GM cars with the front-engine/rear-drive format. Another item engineers wanted was independent rear suspension, but this was dropped for cost reasons. It might have added $600 or so to the retail price, which was considered unacceptable given present market conditions. With a properly located, trailing-link live axle, the irs may not really be necessary anyway.

Another way in which the Camaro/Corvette/Firebird will differ is in motive power. In a few years, they will be the only GM cars offered with V-8s. How long these smooth, free-revving powerplants will be around, even in these specialty models, is a big question right now. A lot depends on government fuel economy mandates after 1985, and what happens to gasoline prices in the next few years. Our guess is that the V-8 will be gone by the late '80s. In the meantime, Camaros will still be fast, roadable grand touring cars in the established tradition of the series.

That brings the Camaro story up to date, but it's far from finished. And that's something to be thankful for. Fuel economy mandates, emission controls, and safety legislation couldn't do in the Camaro. After a difficult time in the early '70s, during which most ponycars disappeared, it bounced back to carve out a solid position in the marketplace. Camaro continues winning new converts every year, and remains a success of which Chevrolet Division and General Motors can be justly proud. For a decade, their designers and engineers kept the car alive by successfully overcoming obstacles that eventually hurt so many sporting automobiles.

The signs are that we're now moving on to a saner age. Again GM is mobilizing its formidable talents and huge resources to produce a new breed of cars that will inspire enthusiasts in the future. It seems safe to say that a great many of those cars will be called Camaro. And if you've liked the story so far, stick around. The way we see it, the best is yet to come.

Acknowledgements

The General Motors Design Staff and Chevrolet Motor Division created the Camaro, and kindly helped us to create this book. Our special thanks to Charles M. "Chuck" Jordan, vice-president, GM Design Staff. He not only gave us his valuable advice, but also made it possible for us to use the Design Staff's archives so we could bring you additional insight into the Camaro story. Photographs of the Camaro's design evolution were provided with the gracious and cheerful aid of Floyd Joliet of the Design Staff's Administrative Operations Department.

We are also indebted to J.W. Crellin, Assistant Director of Public Relations for Chevrolet Motor Division, and to Kay Ward of the Division's Public Relations Staff, for their patience and good humor in obtaining photos of production models from the Division's extensive files.

We are particularly grateful to Michael Lamm (of Lamm-Morada Publishing Company, Box 7207, Stockton, California 95207), author of what has become the standard reference work on this subject, The Great Camaro. *Mr. Lamm kindly gave us permission to quote from several of his interviews with key figures in the Camaro story, as indicated in the text.*

Other published sources consulted were Camaro 1967-1970, *edited by R.M. Clark, and* Great Cars from Chevrolet *by R.M. Langworth and the editors of* CONSUMER GUIDE®.

Periodicals surveyed from the period 1965-80 include: Automotive News, Autocar, Autoweek, Car and Driver, Motor, Motorsport, Motor Trend, Road & Track, Sports Car Graphic, Sports Car World, Ward's Automotive Yearbook, *and* Ward's Monthly.

Fellow Camaro Enthusiasts. . . .

The Camaro Club of America, established a few years ago, already numbers several thousand members, and is represented around the world. A growing roster of local chapters sponsors meets, rallies, picnics, concours, and other events for owners of any model Camaro, 1967 to date. Ambitious national conventions are held annually. The Club publications provide free classified advertising to members, local and national news, technical and historical articles, and sources for Camaro parts and advice. For more information write the National Headquarters, Camaro Club of America, P.O. Box 5037, Kansas City, Missouri 64132.